THEOLOGY
FOR
PREACHING
AUTHORITY
TRUTH AND
KNOWLEDGE
OF GOD
IN A
POSTMODERN
ETHOS

Ronald J. Allen
Barbara Shires Blaisdell
Scott Black Johnston

Abingdon Press
Nashville

THEOLOGY FOR PREACHING:
AUTHORITY, TRUTH, AND KNOWLEDGE OF GOD
IN A POSTMODERN ETHOS

Copyright © 1997 by Abingdon Press

This book is printed on recycled, acid-free, elemental-chlorine–free paper.

Library of Congress Cataloging-in-Publication Data

Allen, Ronald J. (Ronald James), 1949–
    Theology for preaching : authority, truth, and knowledge of God in a postmodern ethos / Ronald J. Allen, Scott Black Johnston, Barbara Shires Blaisdell.
        p.   cm.
    Includes bibliographical references and index.
    ISBN 0-687-01717-3 (pbk. : alk. paper)
    1. Preaching. 2. Postmodernism—Religious aspects—Christianity.
I. Johnston, Scott Black. II. Blaisdell, Barbara Shires.
III. Title.
BV4211.2.A394   1997
251—dc21   97-7471
                                                                                                    CIP

97 98 99 00 01 02 03 04 05 06—10 9 8 7 6 5 4 3 2 1

MANUFACTURED IN THE UNITED STATES OF AMERICA

THEOLOGY
FOR
PREACHING

Contents

The monthly meeting of an Indianapolis area clergy group was nearing its end. The president announced the program for next time. "Our speaker will discuss preaching in the postmodern world." Hesitantly, a thoughtful pastor asked, "What is this postmodernism? I had never heard that word until a couple of years ago. I'm not even sure I can spell it. I hear it more and more, but I don't know what it means, much less what it has to do with preaching."

Postmodernism is fast becoming a buzzword in the theological house and in North American culture at large. Yet, this clergy colleague is part of a significant company of people who are aware of postmodernism but who do not know quite what it signifies. The great Enlightenment synthesis was often called the modern world, modernism, or modernity. Aspects of that synthesis (centered in reverence for science, reason, experience, and the empirical method) are questioned by postmodern thinkers. The prefix "post" suggests that postmodernism intends to transcend modernism. But how?

The heart of the postmodern mind-set is awareness of the relativity of all human thought and action.

The precise meaning of postmodernism is not self-evident. The term *postmodern* does not itself evoke a positive vision. A further problem: many authors or speakers who address postmodernism have slightly different understandings of it. There is no singular postmodern point of view.[1] But many people would agree that Charles W. Allen delimits common ground among sundry postmodernists. "To be postmodern is to be constantly and consistently aware of the relativity of all human thinking and acting." In its sharpest form "it is to be suspicious of, and uncomfortable with, words like 'truth,' 'reality,' 'objectivity,' 'reason,' 'experience,' 'universality,' 'absoluteness.' "[2]

The authors of this volume think that a general mind-set is gradually emerging in many parts of North American culture that can broadly be called postmodern. This mind-set is not univocal. It has many different nuances. In its folk manifestations, it is less a tight philosophical or theological position and more a pattern of inclinations by which people understand the world. This postmodern ethos has implications for preaching.

In the postmodern ethos, the preacher helps the congregation name both how the gospel can help create the emerging world, and how postmodernism might inspire the church to reflect on its witness.

Of course, many people in our congregations are still modern. Others resist aspects of both modernity and postmodernity. The preacher speaks in a mixed community of moderns, postmoderns, and people who are aware (sometimes inchoately) of a shift in the cultural breeze but who are uncertain of its direction.

As the worldviews turn, the preacher has a dual calling: (1) To help the congregation name how the gospel can help create the emerging world. At what points is postmodernity compatible and incompatible with Christian faith? At what points does Christian faith challenge (and transcend) postmodernism? (2) To consider points at which postmodern insights might cause the church to reflect on (and reformulate) basic theological convictions concerning God, the gospel, and the nature and purpose of the church and the world.

Community, collegiality, conversation, and respect for plurality and difference are among the values of postmodernism.

The writing team attempts to embody these values. This book is a conversation among three authors who have different points of view on several of the focal issues, and who come to the issues from different locations (theological, social, gender, vocational). At the time of this writing, Barbara Blaisdell was the pastor of Central Christian Church (Disciples of Christ) in downtown Indianapolis, Indiana. Scott Black Johnston is on the faculty at Austin Presbyterian Theological Seminary, Austin, Texas. Ronald Allen teaches at Christian Theological Seminary, Indianapolis, Indiana.

The conversation that follows is structured so that Ronald Allen articulates a position on an issue pertinent to the postmodern ethos. Barbara Blaisdell and Scott Black Johnston respond critically to Ron's statement and articulate their own viewpoints. In chapters 3 and following, Barbara uses excerpts from her own preaching in order to illustrate and supplement her contributions to the conversation.

The book aims not so much to develop a postmodern homiletic (in the sense of integrating a unified perspective on theology, epistemology, and rhetoric for the sermon) as it does to raise issues that are important to preaching in an ethos that is touched by postmodern predilections. The book has a probing spirit and does not aim to speak dogmatically about postmodernism or a homiletic suitable for postmodern worldviews.

Perceptive readers will object that the community of writers in *Theology for Preaching* is not sufficiently diverse. We agree. However, limitations of space and the mechanics of expanding the team seemed to preclude a larger body of contributors. Perhaps this project will help spark other overtly conversational efforts in the literature of preaching.

Chapter 1 raises the question, "What is postmodernism?" and outlines the major ways (including folk postmodernism) in which that notion is understood. Chapters 2 through 7 focus on a specific issue that is central for the preacher in the postmodern situation: (2) authority; (3) truth; (4) how we know; (5) God and God's relationship with the world; (6) the relationship of the individual, the community, the church, and the world; (7) modes of discourse available to the postmodern preacher. In chapter 8, each author contributes a sermon that is annotated to show how the preceding discussion plays into the practice of preaching.

The authors wish to express heartfelt appreciation to several people who have contributed to the writing of this volume. Barbara says, "I wish to thank the members and friends of Central Christian Church (Disciples of Christ) in Indianapolis, Indiana, for providing the time and spiritual support for this project. Without this community of faith, I could not begin to be what God has called me to be."

Scott says, "I am in debt to Kathryn E. Anderson and Amanda Smith, two students at Austin Presbyterian Theological Seminary, who helped immensely with research and editing. Thanks also to W. Stacy Johnson and Cynthia L. Rigby, two fine systematic theologians, whose willingness to welcome a homiletician into conversation and to respond sympathetically to his many questions, has strengthened this project. My thinking on the topics addressed in this book has been continually stretched and deepened by Stanley R. Hall, Michael Jinkins, and Stephen B. Reid. Lunch with these three provides me with a hopeful paradigm for theological community. I am grateful to William Greenway, who read through a draft of this project, and made numerous helpful and provocative suggestions. Bill's trenchant criticisms and enthusiastic support sustained me through the latter stages of editing. I also wish to express my gratitude to Ronald Allen, whose kind and generous attitude made working on this book a pleasant project."

Ron says, "I thank my spouse and five children for being a

community of encouragement and support. I am particularly grateful to Barbara and Scott for their insight, their collegial spirit, their probing questions, their willingness to be honest and confrontative in friendly ways, and for meeting their deadlines. The issues raised in this book are important. On some points, we agree to disagree, and to do so by consent. None of our disagreements is as important as the foundational element that we share: We are sisters and brothers in Christ, in search of the fullest understanding of God that we can have in our time."

Chapter One

What Does Postmodernism Have to Do with Preaching?

A Perspective from Ronald Allen

Postmodern discussion takes place on two levels: (1) in the technical literature of theology and philosophy; (2) in popular forms of folk postmodernism, that is, aspects of postmodernism that manifest themselves in the thoughts, actions, and feelings of everyday nonspecialists in theology and philosophy. I first recall basic eras in Western culture as a setting within which to discuss postmodernism. I sketch broad outlines in the technical discussion of postmodernism in philosophy and theology. I close with remarks about folk postmodernism. Along the way, I note implications for preaching.

Three Eras in the History of Western Culture

In order to help clarify the meanings of postmodernism, we may think of Western culture (especially in Europe and North America) as divided into three eras: premodern, modern, and postmodern.

The *premodern* period extended to the Enlightenment (though premodern societies can be found today in the Americas, Africa, Asia,

Western history can be divided into three eras: premodern, modern, postmodern. Each has its own characteristics, and its own implications for theology, the church, and preaching.

Australia, and other places).[1] In this world, tradition is the primary determiner of meaning. Many premodern communities are aware of the presence of suprahuman realities (e.g., gods, angels, spirits, demons). The cosmos is a living community in which all things are related to one another. Personal identity is corporate: a person embodies the community to which that person belongs. The natural world is alive and responsive to the will of the transcendent realities and to human actions. "Progress" is easing the human quest to survive.

In the premodern church, the preacher typically assumed the validity of the Bible and Christian doctrine. The preacher interpreted the tradition for the life of the community. Christians sometimes disagreed on the proper *interpretation* of tradition, but its validity was seldom in question.

The *modern* period commenced with the Enlightenment and continues for many into the present. The hallmark of modernism is respect for science and logic. The *empiricists* (e.g., John Locke) looked upon empirical observation as the norm for truth; a claim would be judged true when it was verified through one of the five senses. The *rationalists* (e.g., Descartes, Spinoza, Leibniz) "sought logically unchallenged first truths."[2] Although differing in methods, these two schools shared the idea that one could achieve objective knowledge that is valid in every time and place.

In modernity, the communal consciousness of premodernity yielded to emphasis on the individual as the basic human identity. The cosmos came to be viewed as an object, a collection of resources whose purpose was to provide for the comfort of humankind. Many moderns disdained the past as superstitious and primitive.

For the church, the Enlightenment's confidence in objective knowledge opened the hermeneutical gap. How could people trust archaic sources (such as the Bible) as primary guides into the meaning of life when the formative events of the Bible (e.g., the crossing of the Red Sea, the resurrection of Jesus) could not be confirmed through empirical observation or logical deduction? One of the major responsibilities of the preacher was to help the congregation understand how

Christian belief could be credible. The preacher sought to bridge the gap between the prescientific Bible (and Christian dogma) and the modern world.

Significant elements of the Enlightenment synthesis are breaking apart. While elements of postmodern perspectives were already forming in the heart of the modern period, postmodernism has become widely recognized since the 1970s.[3] Postmodernism seeks to transcend modernism.

While postmodernists differ on many points, they share some common perspectives. Postmodernists recognize limitations in modernism's reliance upon science and rationalism. Furthermore, philosophers and social scientists notice that all perception involves interpretation. Human beings cannot gather pure, uninterpreted data. All people relate to the world through ingrained lenses and prejudices that result from race, gender, education, economic and social class, nationality, ethnicity, sexual orientation, political commitment, and religion. Some postmodern thinkers want to recover aspects of premodernity that were lost in the transition to modernity. In recognition of the relativity of knowledge and views of truth, many postmodernists honor pluralism, diversity, and inclusivity.

Two Broad Strands Within Postmodernism: Deconstructive and Constructive

David Griffin identifies two broad strands within postmodern philosophy and theology: deconstructive and constructive.[4] Deconstructive postmodernism, represented by Michel Foucault and Jacques Derrida, rejects virtually all forms of certainty as

Deconstructive postmodernism emphasizes the absolute relativity of all knowledge. Radical deconstructionism acknowledges no universals. It views

all claims to authority and power with extreme suspicion. posited by modernity. Everything that we think we know is a function of our biased interpretive lenses. There are no universal truths by which to interpret reality. Deconstructive postmodernism exposes the biases and oppressive possibilities in all forms of knowledge and power. It rejects authoritarianism and privilege. It results in radical relativity.

Deconstructionism's emphasis on relativity performs positive functions for preachers by guarding against idolatry and by reminding us not to regard any relativity as absolute. It teaches us to be suspicious of abusive possibilities in all texts, doctrines, and practices. It encourages us to reject authoritarianism. It helps us recognize our interpretive grids. Deconstructionism encourages the preacher to respect differing points of view and to probe them for positive values. Indeed, people at several different points on the postmodern spectrum say that deconstruction is a tool that should always be used when engaging life values. Preachers should always ask, Who benefits from this construal of reality? Who is hurt by it? What needs to happen in order to effect a greater equity for all concerned?

But deconstructionism is problematic. It does not offer a positive vision. Deconstructionism "eliminates the ingredients necessary for a worldview."[5] Few deconstructionists notice a contradiction. By denying the possibility of truth, they deny themselves norms on which to base their objections to modernity and their social programs. Further, "the hearts and minds of people abhor a vacuum, into which new absolutisms quickly rush. 'And the last state of that person is worse than the first' (Luke 11:26)."[6]

Constructive postmoderns also critique aspects of modernity. In addition, they articulate positive visions of God and the world. Constructive postmodernism is most well developed in two forms—postliberal and revisionary theologies.

Postliberal theology is represented by Hans Frei, George Lindbeck, William Placher, Stanley Hauerwas, and William Willimon. In previous generations, liberal theology saw one of its primary tasks to be to make sense of Christian faith in the face of modernity. The designation *postliberal* indicates dissatisfaction with that agenda. Postliberals contend that the witness of the Christian community is not to be measured against external criteria (such as empirical observation, logical deduction). Instead, the preacher describes Christian claims as they are expressed in the Bible (and Christian tradition) and helps the church draw out the implications for Christian faith, thought, and action. The community of faith ought to read the Bible as it does any lifelike narrative, recognizing that some of its details are not empirically accurate, but still trusting its description of reality. The preacher does not justify the believability of Christian faith but explains how Christian faith shapes our view of the world.[7]

Constructive postmoderns recognize validity in many postmodern criticisms of modernity. However, they believe that it is possible to assert positive life vision in the postmodern ethos. In theology, postliberals and revisionary theologians represent two different constructive approaches.

The chief virtue of postliberalism is its thoroughgoing Christian orientation. It warns the preacher against easily accommodating to prevailing worldviews. However, it offers few clear criteria to assess the truth of its claims. Its reasoning is circular (a Christian claim is true because the Bible or doctrine says it is true). Postliberals some-

The postliberals propose that the work of theology and preacher is to tell the Christian story with as little accommodation as possible to the prevailing cultural ethos.

times speak blithely of "Christianity" as if it were a singular phenomenon; they do not always provide guidance for mediating between differing (even contradictory) perspectives in different biblical texts, different doctrines, or different communities. The assumption that the Bible and Christian doctrine normatively name the world sometimes makes it difficult for postliberals to deal with texts (or doctrines or practices) that are theologically or morally problematic. Some critics charge that postliberal theology leads to sectarianism.

Revisionary theology is associated with theologians such as David Tracy, David Griffin, Marjorie Suchocki, Henry Young, John Cobb, and Clark Williamson. My approach to theology and preaching moves in this stream. A number of African American, feminist, and liberation theologies are sympathetic to revisionism (even while developing their own angles of view). As the term *revisionary* implies, it seeks to revise (but not entirely reject) major premises of modernity. "Some of the gains of modernity are irreversible."[8]

This form of constructive postmodernism seeks to incorporate postmodern insights into a positive vision of God and the cosmos. It "does not simply carry the premises of modernity through to their logical conclusion, but criticizes and revises those premises. Through its return to organicism and its acceptance of nonsensory perception, it opens itself to the recovery of truths and values from various forms of premodern thought and practice that had been dogmatically rejected by modernity."[9] Several constructive postmodernists wish "to salvage a positive meaning not only for the notions of the human self, historical meaning, and truth as correspondence, which were central to modernity,

> **The theological method of mutual critical correlation is the heart of the revisionary task. It results in a homiletic of mutual critical correlation.**

but also for premodern notions of a divine reality, cosmic meaning, and an enchanted nature."[10]

Revisionary preachers engage in mutual critical correlation. They seek to overcome the hermeneutical gap by *correlating* ancient and contemporary realities. They *criticize* the Bible and Christian tradition from the standpoint of contemporary perceptions. And, they *criticize* contemporary Christian theology and practice from the standpoint of the tradition.

Revisionary theology can easily fall prey to the Zeitgeist. The contemporary world occasionally changes its understanding of the true and reliable, thus causing shifts in the revisionary vision of God and the world. These changes can erode the congregation's confidence, and can even call the possibility of belief into question. The revisionists can easily take uncritical and functionally idolatrous perspectives into their worldview. Indeed, they can easily recreate God in their own images.

Folk Postmodernism

Beyond these important technical distinctions, I notice a growing folk postmodernism in the community I know best—the Euro-American middle class. By folk postmodernism, I mean postmodern outlooks that are voiced and embodied by people who are not familiar with the formal literature and subtle categories of theologians and philosophers.

Many people today are uneasy with reigning authorities and institutions. Suspicions are often vague and inarticulate but powerful. Science is still respected, but it no longer speaks with an imperial voice. Few people assume that new technology is automatically positive; to the contrary, many people are aware that uncritical technological

Many contemporary people exhibit postmodern sensibilities even though they know nothing of Foucault, Derrida, postliberalism, or revisionism. Not grounded in formal philosophy or theology, they are "folk postmodernists."

developments contribute to a spectrum of problems ranging from nuclear weapons to the ecological crisis.

A growing number of people recognize relativity in the scientific method (and empirical observation generally). As a neighbor commented, "One scientist says one thing, and another scientist says something else. I don't know who to believe." Many people are aware (sometimes dimly) of relativities in human perception. At a point of disagreement in our backyard conversation, my neighbor said, in effect, "You may see it your way, but I see it my way."

Yet, many people are haunted by questions about the limits of diversity. Does anything go? If not, what are the principles by which to determine the acceptable and the unacceptable? I frequently lead Bible studies in local congregations; people often say (in one way or another), "I just don't know what to believe anymore." They are asking, "What is true?"

Some people indicate that they come to Bible study in the hope of getting guidance from the Bible into ultimate reality. Interest in the Bible connects with another postmodern motif: an increasing respect for the past and for the guidance it may offer us.

Postmodernity sees a rebirth of respect for the natural world in its own right. This rebirth is born both from the fear of ecocide and from a conviction that nature has its own integrity. Likewise, in many quarters today, the teachings and practices of native peoples (some of whom preserve premodern elements in their communities) are regarded as wise.

Premodern culture was largely oral-aural. Modernity became print-based. Now, the electronic media are returning an emphasis on oral-aural modes of human communication while adding the dimension of visual images, and not giving up the realm of print.

At the popular level, some people are excited by these developments while others are confused, even fearful. What awaits in the postmodern future? While many folk drift toward postmodernism, a significant number actively resist postmodern possibilities. They respond to its relativism and diversity by tightening the boundaries of the good and the bad, the acceptable and the unacceptable. Congregations and denominations are often in tension between those who lean toward postmodernism and those who do not.

David Tracy reminds us that the preacher ultimately aims to make a *Christian* witness. The preacher's first calling is to release the transformative memory of Jesus Christ into the church and world.[11] It does make a significant difference to preacher and congregation if the preacher makes the Christian witness as a deconstructionist, a postliberal, a revisionist, or in some other mode of theology. However, Christian witness ultimately transcends the concerns of these (and other) penultimate movements. The preacher ultimately needs to sort out the points at which the various postmodernisms are instructive or dangerous to Christian witness. We also need to identify points at which Christian witness can help shape, reshape, and challenge postmodern propensities.

> **The preacher is not first a deconstructionist or a constructive postmodernist. The preacher first seeks to make a Christian witness.**

A Perspective from Barbara Blaisdell

I am writing these thoughts on a Shrove Tuesday. Before my work went from outline to computer, the religion writer from the local paper called to ask why my church, an old-line Protestant congregation from a free church tradition, was celebrating Ash Wednesday with an imposition of ashes. Why does there seem to be a renewed interest even in the "free churches" in this ritual so associated with Roman Catholicism and other liturgical traditions? What is behind the increasing fascination with ritual and tradition? The answer in part: We are increasingly a postmodern culture. With that cultural reality comes increasing openness to ancient traditions and ritual. That openness seems to result in a longing for a depth of wisdom that science and technology have not provided. What might have been dismissed as superstitious or unbelievable in the modern era is received with more openness by many people today. What does this mean for the life of the church as it tries to proclaim the Christian gospel?

Perhaps the most helpful contribution I can make to this effort to explore postmodernism and its implications for church life is to describe how I see its impact in the pews and reflect on how preaching might speak to it. That is to say, I would like to explore further what Ron Allen calls "folk postmodernism," its dangers and values for the strengthening of the Christian witness. I will add a characteristically postmodern caveat.

The people with whom I have experience are largely well-educated, middle-class people. They are predominantly (though not exclusively) Euro-Americans. I worship with a population of folks who are neither fundamentalist nor dogmatically liberal. They are very much like what recent church sociologists have called "lay liberals," the vast middle of our country's population.[12] I cannot speak with experiential authority beyond these rather narrow borders.

24

As a local pastor, I am fascinated to watch these lay liberals or folk postmodernists explore their own spirituality and return tentatively to the church. These are people open to the beliefs and opinions of a wide variety of people and traditions. They are likely, while browsing at the local bookstore, to pick up a book on spirituality from a tradition other than Christian. They are far more comfortable with therapeutic language than theological or ethical language. These folks are not in church because they "ought to be." They are in church only if it seems to be a place where this amorphous spiritual longing might be met. Though the spiritual longing may be vaguely defined, it is deep and authentic. And it is that deep longing which provides the problem and the promise for the church.

Many people in today's church, and in the larger culture, have a deep, authentic, but often unfocused longing to understand the meaning of life.

The problem for the church in this context is that the postmodern culture is not supportive of the church (or any institution) for its own sake. The church is a means to an end or it is irrelevant. Folk postmodernists are people with strong individual values, beliefs, and opinions. But because of their individualism, suspicion of institutional authority, and openness to a wide variety of beliefs and opinions in others, they are reluctant to articulate universal claims for those values and beliefs.

The humility and tolerance of such a stance is hardly to be discouraged in a balkanized world like ours. But the inability to articulate universals has led, I believe, to a shallow understanding of community. The profound biblical concept of how we, as humans, should order our lives has been reduced to a collection of interest-group enclaves: the gay community, the feminist community, the environmental community. Ironically, such enclaves can demand an internal conformity that is every bit as doctrinal and polarizing as the most dogmatic sect. Meanwhile they can leave huge and troubling ethical assumptions unexamined amidst the language of personal fulfillment. Charles Taylor puts it this way:

> Talk of "permissiveness" misses [the] point. Moral laxity there is, [but] our age is not alone in this. What we need to explain is what is peculiar to our time. It's not just that people sacrifice their love relationships, and the care of their children, to pursue their careers. Something like this has always existed. The point is today many people feel called to do this, feel they ought to do this, feel their lives would be somehow wasted if they didn't do it.[13]

The search of post-modern people for spirituality, values, and authenticity provides the preacher with a point of entry for the gospel. The preacher can often correlate the gospel with the community's felt needs, and their larger unrecognized needs.

Social critics (Christian and otherwise) have responded to this cultural reality with despair. That is too harsh a reaction. The good news behind Taylor's point is that postmoderns are not valueless. But many postmodern values have not been sufficiently sorted out.

Beneath the suspicion of many contemporary people concerning claims about authority and truth is a deep commitment to an authentic expression of faith. Authenticity is a value rooted in one of the commitments of modernism: human beings are endowed with a moral sense and must therefore take responsibility for what they do and believe. It is not moral to act simply on the strictures of unexamined external authority. There is a treasure trove for the gospel within this cultural context. If the church can help postmodernists examine and articulate their values of authenticity and self-fulfillment in the light of the ancient wisdom of the gospel, we will help them lead more self-fulfilling and authentic lives. Such an articulation will serve to correct wrong and deviant views of the postmodernists' own values. Just as important, it will make their own values more vivid for them, empowering them to live up to them in a more authentic way. I can think of no more relevant role for the church. To paraphrase Howard Thurman, the church would be aiding our Lord Jesus to put a crown on the heads of broken and hurting sinners, crowns they would spend the rest of their lives growing tall enough to fit, making them their own.

Rather than set the gospel in complete opposition to these postmodern values of self-fulfillment and authenticity, the church should be in conversation with those values, trusting that God may be working here. Such a proposal is actually missionary: it seeks to help postmodernists interpret their experience in gospel terms. However, such a proposal assumes some things, all controversial. It assumes that the values of authenticity and self-fulfillment are valid ideals. It assumes that these values can be critically correlated with Christian teaching in a way that does not violate the integrity of the gospel. It assumes that you can make a case for universals. Finally it assumes that such arguments in reason can and will make a difference. In the postmodern era, such things cannot be assumed, but must be plausibly argued. I hope to do so in my contributions to the following chapters.

A Perspective from Scott Black Johnston

Question: What is postmodernism?
Answer: Quentin Tarantino's film *Pulp Fiction*.

Before you rush out to rent *Pulp Fiction* for next Sunday's adult education class, be forewarned: Most of the people exposed to Mr. Tarantino's cinematic vision find it to be disturbing. A Presbyterian pastor recently declared to me, "It is not the sort of movie that I wanted in my head." With an unswerving eye, the camera confronts the viewer with a world governed by acts of sudden, brutal violence. Sexual abuse, drug addiction, and murder are portrayed in an unsettling, and sometimes gleeful, manner. Interspersed between these stark images, the peculiar characters who populate this movie engage in enigmatic conversations; the dialogue swings from being unnaturally lighthearted to being painfully urgent—topics range from the highly intellectual (French philosophy) to the trivial (the price of a milk shake).

The shape of the plot—the manner in which these eclectic elements are fused together—advances the unusual spirit of this movie, reinforcing the fragmented feeling that one gets when viewing it. For as the film switches from one intriguing setting to another, it becomes clear that we are not watching events unfold in a simple chronological order—like a linear filmstrip. Instead, the scenes in *Pulp Fiction* are assembled as a sort of cinematic collage, so, in the end, the movie comes off as a pastiche—a blend of discordant images and ideas destined to provoke anxious questions in the modern viewer. What is going on here? What are the rules that will help me understand? Should I be laughing or weeping? Is this movie about profound truth or superficiality? If you recognize these questions, or are familiar with the attitude of frustration that undergirds them, then you have at least an intuitive understanding of postmodernism. For to be postmodern is to be post-certain.

Postmodernity Is a Context for Preaching

While *Pulp Fiction* and the general social milieu that it depicts probably fall into the category that Ron has termed "folk postmodernism," the movie also reflects some of the central debates in postmodern academia. Compare

Tarantino's fragmented film to a description that Jean-François Lyotard offers of the current intellectual climate. Lyotard, the French philosopher who has become the biographer of this intellectual moment, declares that postmodernity is a "war on totality."[14] Postmodern theorists such as Michel Foucault and his well-known contemporary, Jacques Derrida, aspire to undermine the notion that there are universal categories that provide the basis for our language, thinking, and beliefs. In a postmodern world, concepts such as *truth*, *grace* or *justice* are revealed to be ambiguous ideas—unsteady terms foundering under the weight of multiple meanings. We cannot be certain about the sense of our cherished words or symbols, because their meaning depends not on solid foundations (as we once thought), but on particular historical contexts. In both the academy and our culture, we have entered a time of profound uncertainty.

Above all, then, postmodernity is a context. It is a way to describe the world in the latter half of the twentieth century. Consequently, it is something with which the preacher *must* grapple. Karl Barth, the Swiss theologian who understood preaching to be the reason for doing theology, once commented that "preachers cannot think enough about the people to whom they are preaching."[15] In order to engage in faithful proclamation on any given Sunday, a preacher must have a thorough knowledge of the world in which his or her listeners are attempting to live faithfully. Whether we like it or not, *postmodern* (with all its various shades of meaning) may be one of the most accurate terms for describing our contemporary context.

> **Preachers must attend to the postmodern context. An awareness of the ambiguities and uncertainties that are in the hearts of many Christians can help the preacher retell the Christian story for our time.**

Postmodernity is post-1960s; it is postactivism. As the foundations unearthed during the Enlightenment have crumbled, postmodern society has evolved into a culture of global channel-surfers. Those with sufficient resources can flick from moment to moment, sampling a bit of this culture and a taste of that fad. Consequently, the postmodern world is something that only the wealthy can afford (fine French wine, vacations in Tokyo, theater tickets on Broadway); while the middle class struggles to keep up (Lean Cuisine in the microwave, family trips to Disneyland, a television in the kitchen); and the poor are sentenced to endure (Dumpster-diving, reduced welfare payments, cardboard shacks in front of the White House).

Two Critical Questions (and Responses) for the Postmodern Preacher

Reflecting on this context, Ron asks two critical questions: (1) Do preachers have anything to learn from postmodernity? and (2) Do preachers have anything to say in this time? Both of these questions warrant an affirmative response, yet the first "Yes" should be qualified while the second should be proclaimed!

What does postmodernity have to teach those who preach the gospel of Jesus Christ? Our initial response might be justifiably pessimistic. After all, Christians stake their faithful lives on a foundation—a solid Rock. If postmodernity claims that there are *no* foundations, and consequently, that every idea, text, and belief rests on shifting sand, then is postmodernity a worldview that is antithetical to Christian doctrine and tradition? We must not be too hasty in responding. For in the later half of this century (building on the work of Karl Barth), significant theological energy has been spent exploring the implications of "nonfoundationalism" for theology. Ron borrows the usual terminology to refer to this approach to theology as *postliberal*. A postliberal, or nonfoundational, theological position turns Christian preachers away from justifying their beliefs and practices through anthropological study (which postmodern theorists claim cannot be universalized) to the faithful claims made by a tradition-embedded community. So as postmodern scholars demonstrate that scientific and anthropological foundations are philosophically unattainable, *faith*—a category ridiculed by the culture of the Enlightenment—becomes viable once again. Consequently, postmodern scholars often provide unwitting justification for nonfoundational theology.

In criticizing postliberal theology, Ron suggests, "It offers few criteria to assess the truth of its claims." This is not entirely true. While the postliberal theologian is not interested in having his or her theological claims confirmed **Contrary to Ron's claim above (pp. 19-20), nonfoundational theologians do have criteria for assessing truth claims.** by some *external* discipline (such as psychology or sociology), without question, there are criteria for assaying the truthfulness of Christian claims. Of course, these criteria are themselves the subject of fiery debate. The various strands for determining the truth of Christian witness (e.g., the Bible, creeds, experience, other Christian writings) are constantly being evaluated as to matters of viability, interpretation, and application. This may explain why, although I share methodological predilections with the figures that Ron has labeled *postliberal*, I do not accede to all of their theological conclusions. Still, the existence of these much discussed criteria will prove indispensable when considering Ron's question, "Does postmodernism have something to say to preachers?" For when a preacher contemplates how postmodernism might inform the task of preaching she or he must continually ask, "Is this true? Is this a critique that the Christian faith ought to make of its preaching?" As the book unfolds, Barbara, Ron, and I will explore ways in which postmodernism may prompt Christian preachers to greater faithfulness. At every step along the way, however, we must pause to see whether the Christian faith supports or rejects the proposal at hand.

Does postmodernism have important implications for preaching? Yes. As the apostle Paul demonstrated in Acts 17, even cultural yearnings (for an unknown god) can point in the direction of faithfulness. Consequently, the decisive portion of this project will be to determine when Christian proclamation ought to hearken to valid postmodern concerns, and when we ought to bring a theological critique to bear on postmodernity. Such is the faithful stance taken by the postmodern Christian. For even though the fog of uncertainty has rolled in, we are not lost, destined to cower in anxiety and apathy. Instead, the Christian preacher is called to push on—humbly seeking trustworthy beacons that can illumine our search for God.

Responding to the Postmodern Context

One of the central characters in *Pulp Fiction*, a hit man played by Samuel L. Jackson, always cites an embellished passage from Ezekiel 25 before he dispatches his victims. The assassin speaks the passage from the ancient prophet because he believes (correctly) that the text will stir up fear in the hearts of those he is about to kill. As the movie concludes, however, the Jackson character reveals that he is going to abandon his gruesome occupation. What prompts this change of heart? Curiously enough, the biblical text. In repeatedly speaking the text, the murderer realizes that the text was not written to bring fear to the hearts of the weak and helpless; instead, it describes God's promise of wrath against those who (just like the assassin) prey on the weak. In that realization, he is transformed. So, while it is extremely doubtful that writer/director Quentin Tarantino intended it this way, *Pulp Fiction* contains a parable of hope for the postmodern preacher. In the midst of a chaotic, violent, uncertain world, a biblical text speaks, and above the din, a transformative word is heard.

Authority in the Pulpit in a Postmodern Ethos

A Perspective from Ronald Allen

Authority is "that reality on which confidence and responsible decisions turn. It is a point of reference, the locus of credibility which gives direction and abiding character to human life."[1] In life generally, and in the church in particular, the authorities that we acknowledge formally (de jure) and by practice (de facto) contribute to the character of existence.[2]

In a culture of pluralism and relativity, what is the basis for the preacher's claims? Why should people accept a pastor's Christian witness as a point of reference? The congregation must recognize the authority of the sermon or they will not likely consent to its visions or claims.

Issues concerning authority are inseparable from those of truth and knowledge (subjects taken up in the following chapters). We discuss authority first because it is an umbrella under which to focus on truth and knowledge.

Changing Patterns of Authority

Many premoderns believed that their ancestors possessed wisdom.[3] The task of subsequent generations was to shape life according to the wisdom of the past.[4] Later generations might discuss (and debate) how best to interpret the traditions. But, when adequately interpreted, the traditions themselves were authoritative.

This pattern of authority functioned in the biblical period and in premodern Christian communities. The Bible is a record of how the biblical peoples interpreted and reinterpreted ancient traditions in order to honor the traditions in new (and often vastly changed) circumstances. Creeds, doctrines, ecclesiastical practices, councils, and leaders (especially ordained leaders) helped Christian communities adapt to (and, in the process, to reformulate) the tradition. These joined the Bible as authorities in the church. The call of the premodern preacher was to explain the tradition and to show how it should affect life.

With the Enlightenment, tradition became much less important as an authority. Empirical method and logical deduction replaced tradition as basic sources of authority. The empiricists sought a "foundation in bare, uninterpreted sensations."[5] The scientific method is a classic expression. The scientist trusts that which can be verified through the five senses. The modern rationalists began with "unquestionable first principles."[6] These first principles were "self-evident truths" that could provide the foundations from which to extrapolate other knowledge. Authority derived from those things that could not be doubted. Both the empiricists and rationalists contended that their methods and results were universally valid.

These construals of reality shifted hermeneutics in the modern church into overdrive. Why should modern people take seriously an ecclesial heritage rife with primitive portrayals of reality? An ax head floating on the water? Really? The invisible God could not be the subject of empirical investigation. Some philosophers concluded that God was not necessary as a first principle. The acids of modernity eroded the church's inherited patterns of authority.

In the modern context, the preacher sought to provide a sensible bridge across the hermeneutical gap. The sermon was authoritative when it helped the congregation see how Christian tradition could be compatible with modernity.

The postmodern ethos brings a significant change. To borrow Edward Farley's vivid phrase, the house of authority has collapsed.[7] Whereas modernity sought universally recog-

nized standards of truth, communities in the postmodern setting typically acknowledge that different communities see
truth differently. Human beings cannot achieve pure, unbi-
ased perception of the world. Every act of observation or
logical deduction is filtered through the lenses of one's own
preconceptions, values, biases, and practices.

In a postmodern setting, the preacher cannot simply
invoke an external source (tradition, empirical observation,
or logical deduction) as sufficient basis for the congregation's
assent. The questions of the deconstructionists haunt the sermon. Why should a community identify with a tradition that
seem incredulous to the contemporary mind or that
enshrines precepts that have sanctioned oppression? The
preacher must develop a rationale for why the congregation
should let itself be shaped by the gospel.

An Authority of Promise Through Conversation

Postmodern inclinations provide clues for a believable
model of homiletical authority: respect for tradition and critical awareness of experience. These impulses are in
continuity with strains of premodern and modern perceptions and yet come under postmodern management.
Tradition and experience form an
authority of promise in a context
of critical conversation.

An authority of promise
observes that authority for a
person or a community derives
from the promise that is offered
by a vision or claim for that person or community. People
consent to a vision (or claim)
when they believe that the

*Contemporary
preachers speak
authoritatively when
they show how the
gospel—the news of
God's gracious love for
each and all and the
call of God for justice
for each and all—*

offers the community a word of promise that emerges from a genuine conversation among gospel, tradition, and contemporary experience.

vision will benefit them *and* the world.[8]

For the church, promise is measured by the degree to which ideas or phenomena seem likely to enhance the awareness and working of the gospel in the world. The gospel is the dipolar news that God unconditionally loves each and every created entity and that God seeks justice for each and every created entity.[9] Communities of believers may consider a vision or claim to be promising when the vision or claim offers the opportunity to maximize the knowledge of God's gracious love for each and all as well as to enact justice for each and all.

Tradition. Many in the postmodern sphere regard the past as containing elements of wisdom that were downplayed or lost in modernity. In this vein, Huston Smith describes such elements as "forgotten truth." Where some moderns viewed the past as primitive and superstitious, Smith speaks of the past as "the primordial tradition."[10] The past cannot be exhumed and replicated in the contemporary setting. But many people in the postmodern community believe that people in former times had insights into life that can benefit today's world.

In an environment sympathetic to tradition, the preacher can draw positively on the past. If the Christian tradition (or elements of the Christian tradition) proved beneficial to communities in the past, the pastor might reasonably hypothesize that, when sensitively interpreted, the tradition could offer promise to people in the present.

Christian tradition is not a monolith but includes many resources from the past. By declaring that the Bible is canon, the church indicated that conversation with the Bible is indispensable to its life. But the tradition includes other voices, such as the creeds, formal doctrinal statements, the stories of Christians in other times and places, and Christian practices.[11]

For instance, an authority of promise is clear in the case of Galatians 3:28 (in Christ, there is neither Jew nor Greek, slave nor free, male nor female). This vision of a just community is promising in our world of fractiousness among different races, ethnicities, nationalities, and classes.

The preacher seeks to discover points at which the tradition can be instructive to the present. At the same time, when the church interprets the tradition in the light of fresh insight, the church's understanding of the tradition may be transformed. This process is sometimes called "traditioning."[12] Such reconstruction is consistent with Christian tradition itself. Christian tradition is not a fixed deposit, but records how the church has struggled to express its faith in different contexts. Indeed, it is traditional for the church to reform its understanding of tradition.

The preacher sometimes needs to discriminate between the degrees of promise in different (even contradictory) Christian memories. Some elements of Christian tradition are not commendable. The pastor needs a theological method to evaluate the degree to which elements of the tradition are adequate to the vision of God's universal love and unremitting will for justice.[13] The preacher cannot rely on tradition alone as a source of authority.

Experience. While we take up the subject of experience in more detail in the next chapter, I indicate its place in an authority of promise. Many modern people reduced experience to that which is examined through the five senses.[14] Many postmodern people contend that their perceptions of reality cannot be reduced to clinical observation of sense data. They posit an enlarged understanding of experience to account for the fullness of their awareness. Experience has "a holistic character, implying not just the discernible and describable datum available to any mode of empirical inquiry, but that discernible datum in the full, ongoing context of whatever is involved, whether discernible or not. . . . The scope, in a word, is as inclusive as the datum that would designate all that is."[15] The sermon becomes authoritative as it points to ways in which the gospel offers promise in this expansive understanding of experience.

These observations require two qualifications. First, the preacher needs to be alert to the possibility that the gospel may make available to the congregation unknown (or unnamed) dimensions of experience. Indeed, the gospel may call the community to enlarge or reshape its awareness of its experience. For example, if a congregation is homogeneous and isolated from Christians of different races, ethnicities, nationalities, and classes, the sermon on Galatians 3:28 may aim to help the congregation grow in its awareness of its relatedness to other Christian communities.

Second, the preacher needs to make sense of conflicts between tradition and experience. Since God is omnipresent, experience itself can be a source of the knowledge of the divine purposes for the world. Recent generations might be sensitive to God's vision for the world in ways that our ancestors were not. In such cases, experience may supersede tradition in its promise.

The church is in dangerous water when contending that experience can take priority over tradition. The church is tempted to recreate God and God's will for the world in nothing more than its own image. The Christian community can baptize its own limited (and sometimes damaging) preconceptions, perceptions, prejudices, and practices, and can turn away from more faithful and promising possibilities. As in the case of tradition, the church can be helped by having a vivid theological vision as well as a clear method by which to illumine aspects of promise and threat in its understanding of experience.[16] Even so, the church should be alert to the possibility of diminishing its witness when displacing tradition with experience.

Conversation. Communities with a postmodern orientation value conversation. They recognize that give-and-take often amplifies a community's understanding of a subject. Persons with different angles of perception share them with one another (and challenge one another). In the process, people often see things that they have not seen before.

Dialogue is especially valuable when people are unclear, even confused, about what to think about an issue or how to work through it. Good interaction allows the community to name the subject (and its constituent parts), to identify points at which the people are certain and uncertain, to recognize strengths and weaknesses in various ways of perceiving the subject and acting on it. The fact of the conversation itself often adds authority to the conclusion, especially if the participants are aware that the conversation has been fair to all points of view. At its best, conversation is an act of critical reflection. Adults in the postmodern world particularly value serious critical reflection that helps them discern alternative interpretations of the data and the positive and negative qualities of each.

In a forceful statement, Hans-Georg Gadamer summarizes the character of conversation.

> To conduct a conversation means to allow oneself to be conducted by the object [i.e., the subject of the conversation] to which the partners in the dialogue are oriented. It requires that one does not try to out-argue the other person, but that one really considers the weight of the other's opinion. Hence it is an art of testing. But the art of testing is the art of questioning. For we have seen that to question means to lay open, to place in the open. As against the solidity of opinions, questioning makes the object and all its possibilities fluid. A person who possesses the "art" of questioning is a person who is able to prevent the suppression of questions by the dominant opinion. A person who possesses this art will himself seek for everything in favor of an opinion.[17]

41

David Tracy notices that as a conversation deepens, the freedom of those involved is enhanced as they "notice that to attend to the other as other, the different as different, is also to understand the different *as* possible."[18]

According to Tracy, conversation is at its best when it follows "hard rules." These include:

> Say only what you mean; say it as accurately as you can; listen to and respect what the other says, however different or other; be willing to correct or defend your opinions if challenged by the conversation partner; be willing to argue if necessary, to confront if demanded, to endure necessary conflict, to change your mind if the evidence suggests it.[19]

In conversation, promise usually becomes manifest. People discover (or refine) the value of existing ways of understanding, or they see fresh possibilities.

The sermon becomes authoritative to the degree that the conversation about its visions and claims offers promise to the community. The conversation takes place among the tradition, and the experience of the preacher, congregation, and the larger world. The preacher seeks for the sermon to help the congregation recognize points at which the tradition offers positive possibilities for the experience of people (and the cosmos). The preacher also tries to discern points at which experience calls us to reframe our understanding of the tradition.

But what happens when the community is confronted by two (or more) appealing alternatives? Conversation does not necessarily conclude with a clear sense that one position is promising and another is unpromising. The preacher cannot always step into the pulpit with a sermon bearing the unqualified imprint,

When the preacher is uncertain about how faithfully to interpret a text or situation, the preacher should name the ambiguities and help the congregation

"Thus saith the Lord." Life and Christian perception do not always fall into cleanly defined categories.

live within them, in the assurance that God is constantly with them in their uncertainty.

In such a situation, the sermon's responsibility is twofold. First, the preacher needs to illumine the situation as fully as possible. The preacher needs to help the congregation determine those aspects of the situation that seem relatively more and less congenial to Christian vision and values. Ironically, the preacher is called to clarify the points that are ambiguous. Second, the preacher can encourage the congregation to live within the ambiguity in the assurance that God is ever present and ever working for the good of all, even when the congregation cannot name that presence and work with precision. The preacher attempts to be faithful to all that can be known of Christian conviction while acknowledging relativities in the situation.

To the postmodern mind, an honest statement of ambiguity contributes to the preacher's credibility. For the congregation is often aware (even if vaguely) of unsettled aspects of thoughts, issues, and situations. Pastors who acknowledge uncertainty in Christian interpretation of an idea or phenomenon signal the congregation that they are perceptive and honest. These qualities are valued in postmodernity. The other side of the coin is that preachers need to be careful not to hide from controversy behind a blanket of false ambiguity. Such hiding is unfaithful. Further, when the postmodern congregation discovers that it has been deceived, the community withdraws its respect.

Monological form and conversational content. A sermon can be dialogical in character while monological in form.[20] Reuel Howe differentiates between form and character in these respects. A sermon that is delivered monologically is perceived as conversational when the congregation finds itself

Preachers can speak in monologue, and yet the sermon can have the quality of a conversation in which the congregation actively participates. Given the postmodern emphases on community and mutuality (see chapter 6), this quality is important.

in the sermon—its experiences, its questions, its hopes and aspirations.[21] This quality is possible when the preacher "feels responsible for and responds to the patterns of experience and understanding" of the listeners so that the listeners are "encouraged to grapple with" their perceptions.[22]

John McClure proposes that the process of sermon preparation can involve actual give-and-take conversation.[23] The preacher can invite laity into the study to think about the developing sermon. This allows the preacher to hear the laity's understanding of the issues under consideration. Further, members of the congregation often have insight into a situation or text that deepens or broadens the preacher's views. The congregation feels as though their concerns are taken seriously.

The preacher can also invite others from the tradition and from contemporary settings. In the process, authority will likely emerge as the sermon posits a witness that is faithful to Christian tradition, credible to the contemporary mind, and mindful of its points of relativity and certainty.

A Perspective from Barbara Blaisdell

By what authority does the preacher speak? In the post-modern ethos, the preacher's authority is no longer rooted in his or her office as an ordained person, or finally even as an educated thinker. A preacher's authority for postmoderns rests in his or her ability to persuade the listeners that the vision (or a claim) is right and true and therefore compelling. Authority is rooted in the community of listeners. I make this not only as a descriptive observation. I also intend it to be prescriptive.

Authority ought to be rooted in the community of listeners in dialogue with the gospel and contemporary ideas. This claim can and does cause consternation throughout the church. It can be and is dangerous, for it means that the gospel can be rejected. This claim tends to personalize and relativize the truth. (I have heard people say, "That Bible verse may be true for you, but it isn't true for me.") It opens up all ethical claims on the individual for negotiation and scrutiny and changes the focus from the common good to the individual good. (What is true, right, good for me?) It severely complicates the public witness of the church.

The problem here is not simply that a teaching of the church may be rejected. That has always been the case. The problem for the church in postmodern times is that sincere believers can and do decide that a teaching of the church ought to be rejected, on moral grounds. The consensus of the church in the eighteenth century on slavery was that it was an acceptable and divinely ordained part of the social order. That consensus began to break down in the nineteenth century. On what grounds did the consensus break down? By what authority did the consensus change? By the patient luring of a postbiblical and postcreedal (at the time) enlightenment idea: that human individuals are endowed with moral sensibilities and thereby have moral rights and responsibilities, which include freedom. Authority is rooted in the community of listeners in dialogue with the gospel and the adventure of ideas.

The preacher often walks a tightrope stretched between the authority of tradition (typified by a closed canon) and the fresh leadership of the Holy Spirit. The preacher's dilemma: how to distinguish the leading of the Spirit from nothing more than the Zeitgeist.

45

Obviously, as Ron points out, this is dangerous ground. Balancing the discipline of a closed canon against the lure of the Holy Spirit in contemporary life has long been a challenge in the church. Today the contemporary claims of individualism have been argued to be destructive of community and in opposition to the witness of the gospel. Much of the emphasis of postliberal literature is calculated to stand against the claims of individualism. But a self-centered individualism travesties and betrays the very moral insight that gives it power. Individualism is rooted in the Cartesian demand that each person think responsibly for himself or herself, that any ethical claims upon one's life must be internalized, must make sense to the individual. Few people would find compelling any ethical argument that failed to even attempt to make sense to the listener. Indeed, persons who believe in something simply because it is what they were taught, without reference to their own experience and without conversation with others, lose not only credibility, but also moral authority.

While there are those in the pews who are willing not to think critically for themselves about what is being said, this is hardly to be encouraged. I have had conversations in an adult Sunday school class in which someone will begin a sentence, "Well, the way I was taught . . . " I often respond with questions such as: "Did that teaching ever make sense to you? Does it now? Does it strike you as moral, true, right?" If the only answer that can be provided is circular—"Well, it's just the way I was taught"—the argument loses moral force. As my mother once responded in just such a situation, "Some of us learn to grow beyond the way we were taught."

One of the advances of mod-

The preacher needs to create a conversation in the sermon that helps people think critically for themselves in the light of the gospel in a way that calls for self-transcendence.

ernism that we dare not lose is the ethical claim that one must take responsibility for one's own beliefs. That advance demands that authority rest not in the pulpit or the canon alone, but in the conversation of gospel, preacher, and listening community.

How does a preacher encourage the ethical claim on the listeners both to think for themselves and to attend to the claims of the gospel to transcend the self? The preacher who desires to encourage both must find the connection between both. That connection lies in a fuller understanding of self-formation. The reality is that we cannot think or define or fulfill ourselves by ourselves. We do our individualized ethical thinking dialogically, in conversation with or in struggle against competing definitions of the self. As Charles Taylor says: "Reasoning in moral matters is always reasoning with somebody. You have an interlocutor and you start from where that person is or with the actual difference between you. You don't reason from the ground up, as though you were talking to someone who recognized no moral demands whatever."[24] Not only is ethical reasoning always conversational, it is conversational against a background of things that matter. That is, my choice to do this or that thing only matters if my choice makes a difference, if some choices are better than others. What are the values inherent in the choices of the listener? How might they be illumined and expanded by the gospel? This is the point at which Ron's discussion of the authority of promise is most helpful. *People consent to a vision (or claim) when they believe that vision will benefit them and the world.* Taking responsibility for what one believes, therefore, need not and ought not collapse into a self-absorbed ethic. Taking responsibility for what one believes is an ethic that requires that one converse with the most penetrating of partners. Scripture and tradition are penetrating conversation partners. However, for many postmoderns, they are lost conversation partners. A huge part of the preacher's

Liberal and conservative preachers too often use scripture to cut off homiletical conversation and trump the argument. Experience must also have a voice in the sermon.

task in the postmodern world is to reintroduce them into the dialogue.

One of the implications here is that scripture and tradition, as well as the experience of others and the experience of self, will be partners. This need not imply that all partners are equal. It does imply that all partners are respected and listened to.

Too often in the church and in the pulpit (in liberal and conservative pulpits alike) scripture is used to cut off conversation and trump the argument. Any preacher with experience will know that in a stewardship campaign, preaching that simply argues, "Jesus taught us to deny self, to sell all we have and give it to the poor," will fail. It fails because it is the preacher's attempt to be coercive. People rightly resist coercion. To have authority in a postmodern ethos, a sermon must ponder the complications and competing claims of the wealth we have been given to guard as stewards (e.g., What do I owe the church? What do I owe my children? What are my responsibilities in regard to taking care of and improving myself as distinct from improving the world?). These are honest conflicts that deserve honest treatment. What conversation can scripture provoke?

I find Ron's discussion of the ethical claims implied in such conversation to be extremely helpful. Ron's comments are rooted in the idea that each individual must take responsibility for his or her beliefs, or else conversation is pointless. In this regard, the conversational nature of authority is not primarily a matter of rhetorical strategy on the part of the preacher, it is an ethical demand.

A Perspective from Scott Black Johnston

One day, as he was teaching the people in the temple and telling the good news, the chief priests and the scribes came with the elders and said to him, "Tell us, by what authority are you doing these things? Who is it who gave you this authority?"

Luke 20:1-2

Whither Authority?

Does the Christian preacher have authority anymore? Do people still come to church expecting to hear something true—open to a proclamation that will lay a claim on their lives? Or has the authority of the pulpit all but evaporated? These perennial questions take on an urgent tone in our postmodern climate. As contemporary philosophical skeptics continue to cast corrosive doubt on our traditional understandings of knowledge and truth, *authority* looks more and more like an endangered species.

Actually, the concept has been in trouble for some time. As early as 1961, Hannah Arendt argued that the world was beginning to experience "a breakdown of all traditional authorities."[25] The work of today's postmodern thinkers, however, has quickened this already rapid deterioration, bringing preaching to a crisis point. Can we meaningfully refer to the preacher as "one who speaks with authority" in the current context? An affirmative answer will prompt an immediate (perhaps even more difficult) follow-up question, one that echoes the chief priests and the scribes: What is the source of this authority?

Postmodern theories of language and meaning undercut traditional notions of authority. Consider, for example, the *author*, the paradigmatic *author*ity. From a modern perspective, the author is a creator, a person who brings something

For many postmodern theorists, meaning derives not from the author's intention, but from the way the listeners receive it.

meaningful into existence. Notice the theological parallels: the ultimate authority is God, the one responsible for bringing all meaning into existence—The Author of all authors.[26] As creator, the author holds a certain power (i.e., authority) over the created work; he or she is in a privileged position when it comes to understanding the created text. Those who embrace this approach to authority have a clear way to resolve interpretive debates that arise. When questions of meaning come up, the most reliable (although, not always possible) strategy will be to consult with the author, for as the creator, she or he will always be able to render the most accurate interpretation of a text.[27]

Postmodern thinkers, however, find an author-based understanding of interpretive authority to be egregiously flawed. Texts and words, they argue, do not depend on a creator for meaning. One merely has to look at the way in which the sense of texts, works of art, and even words themselves have changed through history (fluctuating according to different contexts and communities) to conclude that meaning is not fixed firmly in place by a writer, artist, or speaker. Mark C. Taylor, a self-proclaimed postmodern a/theologian, writes, "Everything inscribed in the divine milieu is thoroughly transitional and radically relative."[28] Having established the fickle character of meaning, Taylor and other postmodern interpreters dispense with traditional sources of authority. The creator is no longer needed; the author's intentions can be cut loose from the meaning of a text, and (theologically speaking), the Author of all authors may be pronounced dead.[29] Such resolutions herald a fundamental shift in the locus of authority: from the author to the reader, from the speaker to the listener, and—some would say—from God to people.

Clearly, certain postmodern conclusions concerning

authority prove untenable to the Christian preacher, not the least of which are the renewed "death of God" pronouncements. Yet, some aspects of postmodern theory run parallel to contemporary currents in homiletics and promise to cast critical light on authority. The most significant point of contact exists in the recent emphasis that both postmodernists and preachers have placed on the listener.

Authority and the Listener

In 1971, Fred B. Craddock's groundbreaking book, *As One Without Authority*, became one of the first homiletical texts to advocate for the authority of the listener. Craddock observed that the current generation of preachers no longer seemed to have the authority to "forcefully and effectively witness to the Gospel, initiating personal and social change."[30] While a number of related factors contributed to this crisis, Craddock lay much of the responsibility at the feet of the prevailing approach to preparing and delivering the Sunday morning homily, the deductive sermon. The deductive sermon, argued Craddock, alienated congregations because it did not take account of "the completely new relationship between the speaker and the hearer."[31] Listeners were no longer willing to absorb passively the theological conclusions reached by the preacher each week in his or her study. Instead, Craddock suggested, the listener was eager (in fact, naturally inclined) to play an active role in the making of meaning. So, if preaching was to survive as a faithful Christian practice, the sermon would have to change; it would have to conform to the manner in which people actually experienced life (i.e., inductively). The inductive approach to shaping a sermon encourages the listener to piece together scriptural insights, theological perspectives, and cultural questions, and in the end, equips hearers to draw their own conclusions.

In a postmodern climate, homiletics must reject the idea that all persons listen in the same way. Preachers need to take account of the phenomena that different people receive and process communications differently.

Craddock's proposal was well-timed, injecting new life into the practice of preaching and prompting many homileticians to speculate about the role and authority of the listeners.

Although Craddock's work encouraged a shift in authority toward the listener, it would be inaccurate to conclude that *As One Without Authority* represents a postmodern homiletic. For Craddock based his prescription for the health of preaching on a sweeping understanding of anthropology (that is, all people listen inductively). Postmodern scholars tend to reject such universal claims, and call presumed similarities between "all people" into question. Does *everyone* really listen inductively? Or do different people listen in different ways?

In his book *Is There a Text in This Class? The Authority of Interpretive Communities*, Stanley Fish, a literary critic, provides a postmodern alternative to basing authority in such generalized notions of anthropology. To demonstrate his approach, Fish describes an incident in which he wrote a series of names on a chalkboard in his course on linguistics.[32] Members of the class recognized the list to be a selection of prominent linguistic scholars. When Fish's next class, a poetry class, occupied the same room he drew a box around the list of names and told the students that it was a religious poem; the class then proceeded to provide a rather ingenious analysis of the text as a poem. Fish argues that these two groups of readers arrived at different interpretations of the same chalkboard text because they were following separate "recipes" for making meaning. These recipes—sets of rules—enable communities to interpret the world around them. The particular set of rules embraced by a specific community, claims Fish, provides a basis for a group of people to agree on an interpretation. In other words, these shared interpretive principles establish a framework that determines what is authoritative. So actually, in the postmodern context, authority has not been exterminated; it has been grasped afresh. Fish's work steers us toward the concept's true habitat: in the midst of particular communities and the rules that they share.[33]

A Definition of Authority for the Preacher

So, what does the Christian community mean when it says that a preacher "speaks with authority"? The question remains a difficult one. For clearly, diverse Christian communities construe the authority of the preacher in different ways. Some

> *All authority is derivative. The preacher must ask, "From where does the authority for this statement come?"*

say that the preacher has authority because the Bible undergirds proclamation. Others point to the fact that the preacher has been ordained, and is therefore credentialed to speak of and for God. Still others suggest that the preacher speaks with authority because she or he understands the needs, context, and history of a congregation. Even within the bounds of the Christian community, *authority* persists as a slippery word. Yet, there is a point of congruence that runs through each of these descriptions: they all seek to answer the authority question by pinpointing the source from which it flows.[34] The chief priests and scribes were correct all along: to comprehend *authority* is to understand that it is derivative. We too must ask: From where does this authority come? Taking the context of postmodernity into account, the following definition attempts to identify some of the theological sources from which the Christian preacher derives authority. When we say that a preacher "speaks with authority," we are referring to *the exercise of power by a person called by Jesus Christ to proclaim the gospel to a particular community.*

The Exercise of Power

Preaching is an exercise of power. At its most basic level, this statement acknowledges God's role in the preaching event. Christians confess that the preacher participates in the power of the Holy Spirit—the Spirit of God whose actions bring efficacy to the preached word. Postmodern linguistic theorists, however, push us to recognize that the power of the proclaimed word also operates on other levels.

In tracing the history of ideas, Michel Foucault, a postmodern archaeologist, demonstrates that the meaning of our most important concepts (e.g., justice, sanity, sexuality) have been at the heart of perpetual power struggles. For diverse forces within culture continually vie to define a society's critical vocabulary. Feminist scholars concur, pointing out that the meaning of our most cherished words has always been influenced (even shaped) by persons in positions of authority, those with the power to define legal codes, moral practices, and, indeed, whole ways of life.[35]

When preachers speak, they enter the arena of human power. In describing the world in a theological manner, sermons influence listeners' understandings of God, and consequently, sermons urge people to alter the way they lead their lives. Who can we trust with this vast power?

When preachers speak, they enter this arena of power and become part of the struggle to define the world. In making prophetic pronouncements, interpreting scripture, defining theological terms, and criticizing both culture and church, the preacher influences a congregation's theological perspective. The Christian preacher sits in the humbling position of defining (and also refining) a people's understanding of God.[36] In alerting us to the power of language, postmodern theorists keep preachers mindful of the incredible influence that they wield. Consequently, they keep an important question in front of the Christian community: Who can be entrusted with this power?

The Call of Jesus Christ

The authority by which a preacher seeks to lay claim on the lives of those who listen is nothing less than a summons from God. Without the call of Jesus Christ, Christians cannot speak meaningfully about the authority of the preacher. For Christ, who first called the disciples, is still the one who calls people to preach,

The authority of the preacher is derived from the call of Jesus Christ, and the degree to which the preacher's claims witness to Christ as attested in Holy Scripture.

giving them authority over the powers of the world—authority to act in his name. Christian communities strive to discern this source of authority in the lives of people who would become clergy. Ron has helpfully pointed out that various sources for the preacher's authority have gone in and out of vogue throughout Christian history. Yet, I would argue that Christ's calling is the one source that cannot be missing (it is the *sine qua non*) if preaching is to be authoritative. Indeed, Paul points to precisely this fact in his letter to the Romans, when he asks, "How are they to proclaim him unless they are sent?" (Rom. 10:15).

For the Purposes of Speaking the Gospel

The Christian preacher draws authority from the fact that she or he speaks the gospel. I find this statement to be somewhat distinct from Ron's understanding that the preacher's words are authoritative when they carry a word of promise and benefit for a congregation. Ron's definition needs to be handled with care, for unless we have a rather specific understanding of "benefit," much of what the preacher says may not seem (from the congregation's perspective) to be beneficial at all. For the gospel of Jesus Christ regularly challenges ethical practices that result in worldly benefits. So, while preaching that calls a Christian community to task may be difficult for a congregation to hear, and some may even refuse to listen to such words, that does not mean that the authority of the proclamation is necessarily lacking. A better criterion for testing the authority of the preached word rests in its congruence to the witness of Jesus Christ as attested in the Holy Scriptures. To do this faithfully, a preacher must consider the biblical witness in light of a particular group of listeners.

To a Particular Community

Paying attention to the listener, as Craddock astutely argued, is an essential part of faithful preaching. Indeed, the entire listening community lends authority to the preacher when they are addressed in specific by the preached word. This is not to say that the preacher must make the preached word acceptable to a particular congregation, but it is to argue that authoritative preaching must take account of the congregation's particularities. A sermon based on the text "blessed are you who are poor" (Luke 6:20), for example, may prove comforting to a needy congregation, while it would represent a challenge for a more affluent church. Ron has correctly asserted that "Christian tradition is not a fixed deposit." At their best, Christian communities have reevaluated and applied afresh elements of the tradition in order to respond faithfully to the world around them. This is the continual task of the preacher, the person called to take account both of the biblical witness and the congregation in its context in order to determine what constitutes faithful, authoritative preaching at that moment.

In the end, while Christians confronted by postmodern fragmentation may be unable to pinpoint the "one" way in which preachers speak with authority, we need not panic. We *can* identify sources of authority (Christ and community) and we *can* describe the content of authoritative sermons (gospel-informed and relevant to particular listeners). We *can* discuss the way in which divine power instills the pulpit with holy authority, and we *can* remind ourselves that humans exercise influential power in the act of preaching. Clearly, "authority" has not been vanquished; it persists as a faithful, although polyvalent, term. Indeed, the multilayered character of this definition protects preachers from thinking that we (as the authors of sermons) constitute "the" authority in proclamation. So finally, this definition aims to save us from self-focused certainty to acknowledge the sovereignty of Another.

Chapter Three

Truth in the Postmodern World

The preacher's calling is to tell the truth—about God, about the world, about our communities, about ourselves. But what is truth? How does a congregation know that the preacher is telling the truth? And what is the content of the truth that the preacher is to tell? How can a preacher know if a reformulation of the tradition is a faithful response to the world? These significant questions are knotted with matters of authority and knowledge (discussed in the previous and successive chapters). Premodern and modern pastors responded more easily to these issues than the preacher in the postmodern world of relativism and pluralism. To what degree is it possible for clergy in a postmodern ethos to have confidence that they are telling the truth? Indeed, to what degree is it possible for the postmodern preacher to speak of "truth"?

Truth in Different Modes

In premodern Western societies, truth was largely understood as correspondence between appearance and reality. This notion, now called the correspondence theory of truth, was given pride of place in Plato, Aristotle, and subsequent philosophical discussion.[1] Many premodern folks operated with a functional correspondence notion of truth when they assumed that their tradition was true, and that beliefs and practices that deviated from the tradition were false. The tradition was the source of truth.

The premodern preacher helped the congregation understand how Christian claims conformed with reality.

Premodern preachers would tell the truth by elucidating the tradition and by helping the community discern how the realities of the tradition impinged on the practices of the community.

Two routes to truth prevailed in the modern world. (1) Empirical observation. Science concluded that truth is the correspondence between statement and empirical observation of reality. (2) Logical deduction. Philosophers concluded that truth is logical consistency with necessary first principles. Moderns believed that both routes ended in conclusions with universal validity.

In the modern scene, philosophers sought universal standards for truth. The Enlightenment thinkers sought independent norms that would reveal truth in every time and place. In the modern era, two main approaches became prominent: truth as correspondence, and truth as coherence.[2]

Truth as correspondence was especially important to the empirical method. An idea would be true if it could be confirmed by data received through the five senses. The preacher sorted out those claims of Christianity that corresponded with the empirical view of the world from those that did not. The former were valued and authoritative. The latter could be creatively interpreted or dismissed.

The rationalists introduced the coherence theory of truth. A claim is true (or false) to the degree that it is logically consistent with other ideas within a system of related statements.[3] The preacher would begin with uncontested Christian first principles, and then demonstrate the degree to which other Christian statements cohere with those principles.

The very notion of truth itself has run into hard times in the pluralistic and relativistic postmodern setting. Many deconstructionists explicitly deny the possibility of universal truth. They reason that it is impossible to achieve an objective understanding of reality since all perception is clouded by ingrained biases and by historical context. According to Michel Foucault, and many eliminative (deconstructive) postmodernists, truth is nothing more than a function of power—the prejudices of the most powerful people in a culture raised to the highest possible level in consciousness (often for the purpose of oppression).[4]

In a strange contradiction, however, Foucault makes the normative (and apparently universal) judgment that oppression is uniformly bad. Why can Foucault make this claim when he denies the possibility of universal truth? Nancy Fraser points out that Foucault is simply unable "to account for or to justify the sort of normative political judgment he makes all the time."[5] Chaos, perhaps violence, awaits the world whose respect for diversity allows no standards by which to adjudicate the desirable and the undesirable.

Postliberals eschew using sources external to the Christian faith (such as empirical observation or deduction from first principles) as standards by which to establish truth. The preacher narrates the Christian vision and tries to help the congregation understand how the contemporary community can be shaped by Christian stories, norms, and practices.[6] But why should a community orient itself around the Christian story? Some postliberals make a circular response. A Christian community shapes itself according to the Christian narrative because the narrative is the center of Christian awareness. However, postliberalism moves in the direction of relativism.[7] *Why* should the Christian story be accorded normative status? Why should love and justice be named as normative standards?

Further, one of the irreversible gains of modernity is a nagging desire to know *why* things are the way they are, or why things should (or could) be some other way. Why should a community live in the light of Christian perception? Why not live according to the Buddhist story or the Marxist story or the deconstructionist story? To what standard does the church appeal in order to protest injustice? The functionalist approach of the postliberals does not always answer such questions in a satisfactory way.

A Postmodern Variation on Truth as Correspondence

In the search for truth, the preacher can use the method of mutual critical correlation to determine correspondence between claims and an enlarged understanding of experience.

The preacher can overcome the naiveté of modern views of truth as well as the relativities of deconstructionism and postliberalism by turning to a modified version of truth as correspondence. The pastor can account for the bonafide relativities (especially in regard to perception) that are recognized by the postmodern consciousness. The way forward to truth contains two elements. The first is an enlarged understanding of experience that is characteristic of many in the postmodern ethos, tempered with the awareness that all experience is interpretive. The second is the theological method of mutual critical correlation.

Bernard Meland writes sonorously of the enlarged understanding of experience. Lived experience

> takes on holistic character, implying not just the discernible and describable datum available to any mode of empirical inquiry, but that discernible datum in the full, ongoing context of whatever is involved, whether discernible or not. As a total datum of reality, it is inclusive of whatever is to be apprehended, embracing an ultimate reference along with the

immediacies of recognizable occurrences. The scope, in a word, is as inclusive as the datum that would designate all that is.[8]

Building on the thought of William James and Alfred North Whitehead, Meland points out "that perceptual experience is a richer event than conception can possibly be, providing every occurrence of awareness with a 'fringe,' implying a 'More,' much of which persistently evades conceptualization."[9] Perception of the More (with its vast and powerful depths) is often nonsensory, but it is crucial to the self-understanding of individuals and communities.[10] Conscious interpretive categories cannot exhaust all that we know. Indeed, conscious interpretive categories are only the tip of powerful undercurrents of feeling and force that affect the self and community.

We do not, however, have access to uninterpreted (prelinguistic) experience.[11] In a memorable sentence, Whitehead points out that all experience is interpretive. "If we desire a record of uninterpreted experience, we must ask a stone to record its autobiography."[12] Every moment of awareness, no matter how dim or unfocused, is filtered through interpretive lenses. These lenses are ground by culture, gender, race, ethnicity, family, class, education, political orientation, psychology, religion, ecological setting, our personal histories of feeling. As selves and communities, we

Experience may not be universal. But it is still the experience of particular communities. As such it is a norm against which to measure truth claims. Is a statement true to the experience of my community? If so, I can rely on it. If not, I need to rethink it. Of course, the experience of other communities may cause me to rethink my own understanding

*of experience.
Interpretation and rein-
terpretation are
constant in the process
of relating truth and
experience.*

experience within the context of an interpretive worldview.

When I speak of experience I do not have in mind a pure state of objective perception. I refer to our full range of interpretive apprehension—conscious and unconscious—of the world. The experience of a particular person or community may not be universally shared by all. But it is still the awareness of that person or community. As such it provides a standard against which claims can be measured. Is a particular assertion consistent with my framework of perception? If an assertion is not consistent with my perceptual world, I likely cannot rely upon it.

However, a claim from outside my immediate awareness may push me to realize that my interpretation of my experience is inadequate. I may come to regard my experience differently than I do at present as I become aware that experiences of others open new possibilities for me and for my community. The claims made by other people can cause me to reframe my own perception. This understanding of experience gives me a standard with which to begin assessing claims to truth, but it allows for the relativities in our apprehension that have been uncovered by postmodern theorists.

The preacher aims to explore how Christian claims correspond (or do not correspond) to both sensory and nonsensory experience. This perspective has immediate importance to the preacher. In a study of people who regularly hear sermons, Hans Van Der Geest found that listeners are most likely to regard a preacher's claim as true when the claim is supported by "evidential experience." Evidential experiences are accounts from real life of persons or situations in which the preacher's claim proves true.[13]

At the same time, the pastor must be aware that apparent correspondences (and noncorrespondences) are themselves historically conditioned and subject to revision. The preacher who tells the truth in a postmodern community always mediates between two points of awareness. At one pole, to recast an expression from 1 John, preachers speak of "what we have heard, what we have seen with our eyes, what we have looked at and touched with our hands, concerning the word of life" (1 John 1:1). The postmodern version would add, "and what we have felt in the depths of life." At the other pole, preachers need to recognize that their interpretations are precisely that: interpretations. We have not seen, and heard, and touched, and felt all that can be seen, and heard, and touched, and felt. My limited and biased faculties of perception and intuition can never reveal the utter fullness of the given. Interpretations can change in the presence of fresh data, perceptions, or questions.

The congregation is most persuaded of the truth of a claim when it is confirmed in the life story of a person or community with whom they can identify.

This approach makes it possible for preachers to make their way through the tension between the search for universal claims for truth and the fact that experience is always particular and contextual. Preachers can speak with confidence even while acknowledging the relativity of their claims. As Charles Birch (a scientist-philosopher-theologian) puts it, "Dogmas we don't need. Convictions we do need. The difference is that dogmatists are not willing to be challenged. Those who hold convictions without being dogmatic are willing to be challenged."[14]

When confronted by contradictory claims, the preacher should set up a conversation to evaluate the degree to which the differing claims cohere with the heart of the Christian vision and with the experience of the community.

When confronted by different (even contradictory) visions, the preacher is called to have a conversation to probe for those aspects of each vision that seem most, and least, correspondent with experience. The preacher tests Christian claims against the experience of people in other contexts. At the same time, the preacher must be willing to test the viewpoints of others in Christian experience. The preacher commends those that seem most plausible and raises questions about those that seem least plausible.

Pastors are sometimes called to preach beyond their own experience.

Furthermore, as Joseph Sittler points out, pastors must sometimes preach beyond their own experience. Sittler likens the preacher to Moses on Mount Nebo prior to his death; Moses can see the promised land, but he does not enter it. Nonetheless, he interprets it from afar. Like Moses, the preacher must sometimes speak Christian truth that is not a part of the preacher's immediate world on the strength of the testimony of others.[15]

The preacher probes for the truth by means of the mutual critical correlation of Christian vision and experience.[16] The pastor attempts to correlate a Christian claim with the congregation by showing how Christian perspective is manifest in the full experience of the community. For instance, Romans 6:3-4 asserts that those who are baptized into Christ "have been buried with him by baptism into death, so that, just as Christ was raised from the dead . . . so we too might walk in newness of life." The preacher can confidently proclaim that this text is true because she knows persons who are baptized in Christ and who experience newness of life. The claim of the text corresponds to the experience of the congregation. The preacher's task, then, is to help the congregation discern the trustworthiness of the text (and of Christian baptism) and the implications of newness of life for the believing community.

To tell the whole truth, of course, the preacher must acknowledge that not all who are baptized appear to experience immediate newness of life. This case does not refute the claim of the text. Rather, it may point to something missing in the perceptual awareness of the candidate. Perhaps the candidate was inadequately prepared to receive baptism. (The candidate needs to know, for instance, that baptism does perform magic.) Perhaps the candidate does not perceive nuances of newness that God offers. For those baptized at early ages, such recognition sometimes comes a long time (even years) after baptism. Perhaps the candidate expects an immediate change of life circumstance when baptism promises a change of perspective within which to experience all of life circumstances. An unemployed person who enters the waters of baptism may not get a job, but baptism ought to assure that person of the constant companionship and support of God through the time of unemployment, even as God is working to bring about a world in which all have honorable work. The preacher needs to help the congregation understand the nature of the promise of the text by showing the nature of baptismal new life.

A homiletic of mutual critical correlation also requires the preacher to tell the truth by showing how our awareness of experience causes us to reformulate, or even reject, aspects of the tradition. The experience of God as unconditional love causes me (and many others) to believe that some texts in the Bible, and some aspects of Christian doctrine and practice, do not represent the best of our knowledge of God when they authorize the mistreatment of other human beings or the earth itself.

While the church must sometimes preach against a text, doctrine, or practice, such elements should be kept in the memory of the Christian community to help the church continually remember its finitude.

67

A caveat comes with the possibility of reformulating or delegitimizing elements of Christian vision. No matter how untrue (or otherwise problematic) these materials may be, the church needs to remember them. Their presence, even when delegitimized, reminds the church that repressive possibilities can be found in the Christian house; the church needs continually to exercise at least a measure of suspicion with respect to every aspect of the Christian worldview in order to minimize repression and falsehood.

The presence of difficult material is a continual reminder of the church's finite field of perception. We cannot absolutize (much less idolize) postmodern perspectives. While it may be difficult to imagine now, the church may someday come to believe its delegitimation of some aspect of Christian tradition is itself illegitimate.

The preacher needs to employ the method of mutual correlation very carefully. Claims, visions, and stories may be untrue in one mode of awareness, but true at another.[17]

For example, the Deuteronomic theology holds that a community is blessed when it is obedient to God but cursed when it is disobedient. These claims are not true if a community understands blessing and curse in simplistic material terms. Every reader of this book knows people who are faithful but who are not materially blessed. We also know people who are unfaithful but who seem to prosper in every material way. Our experience does not confirm the generality of the text at the surface level. This argument from experience is not new. The sages of the biblical world (e.g., Job 2–19) wrestled in a similar way.

But at a deeper level, the text is true. Those who are obedient can experience a significant dimension of the blessing of God in the sense that they are aware of being in harmony with divine purposes in the world and empowered by the divine Spirit. Such faithful people may not know the fullness of material blessing that God intends for all. But they can have the blessed satisfaction of being in league with the divine. I cannot say with certainty that prosperous, disobedient people regularly recognize a dimension of curse in their world. But persons who have been unfaithful and flourishing, and who have returned to God, sometimes testify that despite their prosperity, they felt that something was missing from their experience. The full truth, of course, is that God wants all to live in the full state of blessing, material and transmaterial, and that God wants none to experience the alienation of the curse.

Rubrics for Telling the Truth from the Pulpit

The postmodern version of truth invites three rubrics for the pulpit. These help both preacher and congregation maintain a clear line of sight on the sermon and its claims. When these qualities are present, I think the congregation is likely to be particularly open to the sermon.[18]

The homiletic of mutual critical correlation is marked by honest discussion of the issues, humility in the face of our finite perceptions, and critical openness to other notions of truth.

1. *Honesty.* The preacher needs to tell the whole truth. As we have seen, pastors should have much to affirm as they explore correspondences between Christian claims and the experience of the community. The preacher must sometimes challenge the congregation to stretch its understanding of God, Christian vision, and life. However, the preacher needs to be equally honest about questions and points that are not resolved. The integrity of the preacher, the sermon, the church, and the Christian witness require as much.

2. *Humility*. Of course, postmodern preachers want to tell the truth with confidence. Preachers in the postmodern setting ought to recognize that their understandings of truth are limited. Postmodern ministers recognize that their interpretations of truth are *interpretations*. This awareness should take away any arrogance, authoritarianism, or imperialism.

3. *Openness*. Postmodern preachers need to be aware that new angles of vision may revise their present interpretations of tradition, experience, and truth. The preacher is open to the possibility that encounters with others may expand, shrink, refocus, or refashion current notions. Such openness does not mean that the preacher will baptize every new perception that walks through the door of possibility. The adequacy of new perceptions must be tested. But a preacher who is open to postmodern possibilities will not automatically regard a stranger as one to be feared. Even if pastor and people cannot endorse the other, they can be enriched by the encounter. At the least, they have a better appreciation for their own worldview and practices. The community may even be genuinely changed.

Whatever the outcome of the encounter, preachers who are living into the postmodern setting realize that they have not "arrived." They have reached a point that is the start of a new series of reflections on the degree to which the community's current interpretation of the Christian vision tells the truth.

A Perspective from Scott Black Johnston

What is truth? said jesting Pilate, and would not stay for an answer.

(Francis Bacon, paraphrasing the Gospel according to John in Of Truth [1625]*)*

The Center

The manner in which *truth* is handled in the contemporary world reveals more about postmodernity than any other single concept. Almost everyone agrees that truth is important; Christians unanimously concur, "Preachers ought to speak the truth." Yet, this initial agreement provides only a scant veneer of civility—boxers nodding to each other before a vicious battle. For when truth is at issue, other weighty concepts (such as authority, knowledge, community) hang in the balance.

Knowing this, groups that wield (or hope to wield) power within a society vigorously promote their particular understandings of truth, so that whenever Pontius Pilate's famous question is posed, the gloves come off. Within the church, recent arguments concerning divorce, abortion, the ordination of homosexuals, the meaning of justice, and the authority of scripture demonstrate all too clearly that Christians cannot agree on what constitutes truth. Pointing to this confusion, postmodern scholars simply smile, for the church provides another concrete example of one of their primary assertions: In the postmodern world, *truth* is a fragmented concept that can no longer be easily identified.

What is truth? Traditionally, the branch of philosophy that considers such questions of ultimacy has been called metaphysics. According to the postmodern theorist Jacques Derrida, the history of metaphysics is the history of the various names and metaphors that people have used to describe the organizing principle that lies at the center of life.[19] Metaphysicians argue that this fundamental principle (e.g., reason) provides the basis for our meaningful structures (i.e., languages, economies, even cultures). The center of any particular structure determines, encourages, and limits the meaningful practices and patterns that arise from it. For

71

example, if the principle of capitalism lies at the center of an industrial company, then that company, whether it makes automobiles or ice cream, will be structured to make a profit. Of course, at the level of metaphysics, theorists are not interested in the structure of corporate units, but in the very patterns of the universe.

The question of "What is truth?" can also be phrased, "What is at the center? What is the foundational core that organizes our lives?"

Many of history's most important thinkers have debated the identity of the fundamental principle(s) at the center of totality; indeed, a continual stream of Western philosophers have argued for the merits of one such "first principle" over others. Enlightenment scholars suggested that the structure of the world rested on the bedrock of rationality and logic. Offering a different option, philosopher Martin Heidegger argued that the central thing that we have to build upon is the givenness of human existence—our Being.[20] Karl Marx pointed to economics as being primary. Over the centuries, a myriad of other names for the center of totality have been put forward, including God, consciousness, experience, love, and justice.

Studying these many proposals, it becomes apparent that another way to ask "What is truth?" is to ask "What is at the center?" On what foundational core do we depend to shape the meaning of our lives together? These inquiries are not confined to the philosophical community. Increasingly, those sitting in the pews pose similar urgent questions. "What can we rely on in this world? Is anything ultimately true?" In fact, postmodern rumors about the instability of truth have intensified people's thirst for a reliable center. For as Derrida observes, "The notion of a structure lacking any center represents the unthinkable itself."[21]

The Rupture

Derrida, however, is unwilling to indulge our need for a reassuring core at the heart of our structures. Instead, the philosopher endeavors to disassemble our traditional understanding of the relationship between a structure and its center. The concept of structure, he argues, has experienced "a rupture," for it is no longer clear that there is any connection between our proposed centers and the structure of totality. Derrida claims that two contradictory impulses —each pulling against the other—have opened this devastating fissure. The first impulse is our desire for a center—our search for trustworthy ground on which we can securely stand.[22] A second, related impulse prompts us to describe this center. We want to form an accurate picture of the core that transcends our structures. Consequently, Western thinkers have proposed an abundance of different descriptions for the center, and when one description has proved to be inadequate (e.g., God), we have been quite willing to seek a substitute (e.g., rationality). "The entire history of the concept of structure," states Derrida, "must be thought of as a series of substitutions of center for center."[23] Derrida views this swapping of centers with great suspicion. For as one center is exchanged for another, it becomes increasingly doubtful that the center is what gives rise to the structure. In fact, the structure begins to look remarkably stable next to the center du jour. Pointing to the fact that the structure of totality marches on even as we suggest an infinite number of substitute centers, Derrida declares that, despite our unending desire to posit one, *there is no fixed center.* In doing so, the philosopher moves beyond the modern question, "What is truth?" to the postmodern question, "Is truth possible?"

73

Two Trajectories

In pronouncing the center to be absent, does Derrida pull the plug on the concept of truth? There are at least two trajectories that one can pursue in answering this question. The first trajectory follows the lead of Mark C. Taylor, who makes considerable use of Derrida's writings in his book *Erring: A Postmodern A/theology*. "Postmodernism," writes Taylor, "opens with the sense of *irrevocable* loss and *incurable* fault."[24] According to Taylor, this "fault"—like Derrida's rupture—opens a gap between our words and any foundational core which might ground their meaning. Cut loose from the idea of rational foundations and transcendent referents, our words are revealed to be "irredeemably shifty" and floating in an "endless drift of meaning."[25] There are no constants and no truths.

Taylor's work casts the role of the preacher in an alarming light. For if Taylor is correct, Derrida has opened a chasm between the pulpit and the pews across which meaning and truth are unable to travel. In the end, Taylor's scenario would banish preachers to a homiletical Babel in which God is dead and our words have become futile signs wandering in a labyrinth from which there is no exit.

Fortunately, an alternative trajectory emerges when reading Derrida's work with theological eyes. For while Derrida clearly contends that we do not have access to a center that is fully present to us—a foundational core that gives rise to all our words and practices—neither does the philosopher argue that this center is utterly absent. Instead, Derrida prefers to speak of "a trace" and "a shadow"—a partial presence that stands beyond our self-manufactured centers—calling our assumptions about totality into question.[26] In fact, within Derrida's writing, there is an appreciation for what can only be termed *mystery*—an aspect of truth that preachers would do well to contemplate.

Where Is the Center?

Christian preachers will always be more intrepid in naming the center than Derrida would find philosophically comfortable. Such is the nature of our vocation. We are called to proclaim the truth, and the truth that preachers have to speak is Jesus Christ. Nevertheless, Derrida's work puts salient and therapeutic questions to our confession. Who is this

Jesus Christ is the center of the Christian life. Christ is the norm against which to measure all other centers of meaning and behavior. Indeed, Christ sets a question mark against all other centers.

Jesus Christ? What is the nature of this gospel truth? These inquiries are critical, for throughout history, the truth of Jesus Christ has been claimed as the sponsor of both fantastic and horrible things.

In the face of this regrettable dimension of our history, Derrida's writings can shake us free from a dangerous sense of security. For he prompts us to consider the character of Christ's gospel: Is it a religious truth that, like any other truth, sits at *the center* of a structure, giving rise to and supporting ecclesial activities in the world? Or is the truth of the gospel like the mysterious presence of our God, a truth that frequents the outskirts of our structures, calling both the ways of the world and the practices of Christ's church into question? Karl Barth suggests an answer, for the Swiss theologian recognizes that Jesus Christ is not simply another entry competing to describe the center of totality. As he puts it, "The gospel does not exist as a truth among other truths. Rather, it sets a question-mark against all truths."[27] Clearly, this is a risky proposition, an approach to truth that will seem threatening to many elements of the church; and yet, it is consistent with the parabolic teachings of the New

Testament Jesus. For time and time again, the scriptures tell of Christ calling established structures and norms into question by providing unconventional images and metaphors for God's realm.

When the gospel of Jesus Christ is preached in the contemporary world, it maintains this unsettling demeanor, and preachers and congregations alike find their limited expectations and finite structures overturned anew. For the character of the gospel means that the center is not always where we expect it to be—a stationary object beneath our theological crosshairs. Instead, it is a moving, mysterious truth, active in the world, refusing to be pinned down, calling us to faithfulness.

Preaching God's Truth

The nature of God's truth in Jesus Christ provides both a caution and a challenge for the preacher in the postmodern world. First, it cautions pastors against homiletical arrogance. Preachers occupy a tenuous position. We are called to preach, but we know that our words cannot capture the fullness of God. This, according to Barth, is our affliction.

> As theologians, we ought to speak of God. We are, however, human beings and as such cannot speak of God. We ought to recognize both our obligation and our inability—and precisely in that recognition give God the glory. This is our affliction [Bedrängnis]. Everything else is mere child's play.[28]

The preacher's predicament, as Ron has pointed out, requires that an attitude of humility infuse faithful proclamation. For ultimately, the truth of our preaching is not dependent on our rational ability to uncover and dispense the gospel, but on the promise and activity of God.

God's involvement in Christian proclamation also provides

preachers with a significant challenge. How do we know when we speak the truth? Suggesting that a preacher's claims are true when they are "verified by what really happens in the world," Ron argues that we can identify the truth within human experience. Certainly, there are many times when events in the world will support the Christian preacher's words. Still, we might well wonder whether a Christian claim becomes true only when it corresponds with the experiences of listeners. For as

Christian preachers cannot limit their claims about truth to those that correspond with experience. Because preachers speak of a God who is transcendent as well as imminent, we necessarily have more to say than can be verified by present experience.

Eberhard Jüngel puts it, "Religious language necessarily accords to actuality more than an actual state of affairs can show of itself at a particular time, more, indeed, than it is capable of showing for itself at any particular time."[29]

This is not to say that Christian preaching should avoid speaking about human experience. Indeed, we are compelled to speak about people's experience both of the world and of the divine. In so doing we perform the vital task of placing human lives in conversation with the transforming truth of God. Yet, precisely because the Christian preacher must speak of God—if she or he wishes to speak the truth—the preacher will always have more to say than experience will bear out, than reality will seem to support.

This discussion brings us back to Pilate, a person who expected the claims made about Jesus to be confirmed by his experience. In asking his metaphysical question, "What is truth?" the Roman procurator was looking for a solid foundation on which he could base a judgment. Ironically, of course, the very systems, structures, and foundations at the center of Pilate's experience were being called into question by the incarnation of truth standing there crowned before him. The challenge of Christian preaching is the challenge presented by Pilate. Will *truth* remain simply an object, something that we can be certain about, some "thing" that we can study at the center of our finite systems, or will truth be understood as an active subject—God on the move? In a rational world where people seek a stable center that will provide a foundation for their experience, we are called to proclaim the truth of Jesus Christ, which by its very nature undermines our notions of security and would, by mysterious means, transform our experience of all that is.

A Perspective from Barbara Blaisdell

Scott Black Johnston, in his contribution to this chapter on truth, rightly demands that those of us who seek to preach in the postmodern milieu use a hermeneutic of suspicion when making any truth claims. Passionate defense of the truth has been the occasion for terrible crimes against humanity. Truth claims can and are used to secure and protect power. In addition, in our diverse society, we are increasingly aware that there are widely differing understandings of the foundations for truth. Does this mean we cannot speak the truth? Johnston argues that we can, if we attend to the reality that truth is always moving and mysterious. He writes, "For ultimately, the truth of our preaching is not dependent on our rational ability to uncover and dispense the gospel, but on the promise of the activity of God." This looks suspiciously like a rationally accessed truth claim to me. And it begs the question: How do we know if what we are dispensing is the result of the promise and activity of God or of some less benevolent power (such as our own sin)? How might we discern the difference between the promises of God and the promises of evil?

I agree with Ron that a preacher can overcome both the naiveté and narrowness of modern empirical views of truth without an equally narrow appeal to mystery. The preacher searches for and seeks to articulate the truth by bringing the claims of the gospel into conversation with the deepest moral intuitions that arise out of human experience. There is mystery here, but it is mystery as a tactical problem: we cannot see all we need to see in order to discern the whole truth, once and for all. To paraphrase Meland, we live more deeply than we can argue or articulate. Therefore, we must be humble and willing to listen whenever we speak.

Preachers must have criteria by which to assess whether their messages portray the promise and activity of God, or some lesser power.

But if we think something is true, then it matters to be able to say it. Some appeals to mystery function as a strategy for living. (For example, I hear people say, "We cannot know the ways of God. They are mysterious to us.") Such an appeal undercuts our ability to make any claim. It removes the search for truth from the realm of public conversation, making community impossible and preaching irrelevant. If Barth is right, and we as human beings cannot speak adequately of God, then we ought to shut up. Otherwise our truth claims become a private intuition about the depth of life and the glory

If preachers cannot speak adequately of God, we ought to shut up.

and activity of God. Merely private intuitions are removed from the rigor and corrective of conversation.

I find mutual critical correlation between contemporary ideas, our deepest apprehensions of experience, and the claims of the gospel to be marvelously felicitous for making a case for truth. The conversational model recognizes that the Christian witness (in both scripture and tradition) is filled with morally troubling claims, and it gives the congregation some norms for choosing between those claims. This method does not promise to give the whole truth for all time. It does allow preachers to say why we believe what we do, and why a congregation ought to listen.

As a preacher in a local congregation, I long to see examples of how these issues (and other issues raised in this book) come to expression in sermons. We provide sample sermons in chapter 8. However, in order to prefigure how these theoretical discussions affect actual preaching, I include excerpts from my own preaching in this chapter and in my contributions to subsequent chapters. In Fred Craddock's evocative image, I try to move my discussions from that of a book that a preacher would read on Monday (one that provides theoretical perspective and important background and framework) to a book that a preacher would read on Thursday (one that moves to direct homiletical appropriation). Along the way, I comment on how the perspectives of Ron and Scott intersect with the sermon.

An excerpt from a sermon shows how a Christian understanding of truth regarding God's relationship to persons with HIV/AIDS results from a homiletic of mutual critical correlation in which Christian tradition comes into conversation with the contemporary experience of HIV/AIDS.

The following argument was made from my pulpit. It brings the nature of the gospel to bear on the HIV/AIDS pandemic, and points out the wildly conflicting truth claims of the church regarding the theological implications of this issue. It attempts to provide the congregation with resources for testing the veracity of those claims against their experience, their deepest moral intuitions, and the gospel.

Showing the world the love of God is what Jesus Christ asks us to do as a church. He sends us into the world, to tell the world about the love of God, as he has shared it with us. He sends us out to be a sign of the kingdom of God in which God's unconditional love rules. It is our primary task as a church not to give testimony to judgment and hate, but to give testimony to that divine love. This is especially important these days, because evil has gotten a hold of parts of the church, causing parts of the church to do exactly that which Christ called us not to do: to proclaim a hateful god rather than a God of grace and love, the God of the cross. Some in the church have declared that the HIV/AIDS epidemic is the result of the will of God, that there are people God so hates that God wills that they die from this horrible disease. What is at stake here is not simply our ability or inability to love persons with HIV or AIDS. What is at stake is what the church says about God's ability or inability to love.

Now, for those of you who do not know our Disciples of Christ tradition, let me tell you how we come to understand what is true about God. We take the Bible very seriously. We do not take it literally. We are not surprised to find things in scripture that offend us as well as things that uplift us. There are profound truths in this book. And there is stuff in it that human beings, being who we are, have used as weapons to hurt those whom we fail to love. This is holy, sacred scripture. To use it for hate is to abuse it. Anyone who uses this book to beat you up emotionally has no authority from God. God does not ordain bullies. We take the scriptures seriously—and seek to understand them in the context of love.

The second way we come to understanding the nature of God is by using our hearts and minds

We come to understand God's truth about HIV/AIDS by interpreting the Bible and our tradition in a context of believing that God's love is unconditionally for each and all, and by using our minds and hearts to reflect deeply on our experience.

81

to reflect deeply on our experience. This is no easy task either. For this world can be a nasty place. And if you have been raised in that stream of life that says God is a kind of divine air traffic controller, choreographing all our takeoffs and landings, responsible for everything that happens to us, and then you find yourself in the wreckage of one of life's crashes—well, any good heart and mind reflecting on the airports of this world will come to the conclusion that the giant air traffic controller in the sky is either napping, negligent, or just plain mean.

This point is where our scripture and our deepest experience can begin a kind of dance in our imaginations—and help us understand. The biblical texts read today (Psalm 91, Deuteronomy 32:11-12, Luke 4:31-37, 13:34b) describe God not as an air traffic controller, protected behind glass, high in a tower above us all, manipulating the world on a divine computer. Rather, God is compared to a living, soaring bird, a mother eagle, and Christ calls himself a mother hen. We are the offspring making our first ventures out of the nest. The chaos and danger of the larger world are real. The eagle is not above it all, behind control tower glass, but is out here with us. When life's storms come, scripture tells us that God seeks to gather us, protect us underneath God's wings. And when we attempt to fly, and instead start to tumble toward the ground, scripture says our eaglelike God swoops beneath us to catch us, and to raise us up to soar once again.

Does this sound improbable or sentimental to you? It may well—because many of us here today do not feel at all protected by God. Part of the evil of illness and suffering is its ability to isolate us, to make us feel abandoned, all alone. And part of the way the evil of illness works to isolate us is to play on our guilt and fear. It is a universal human tendency: when we get sick, or when something

bad happens, we search our memories for what we have
done to deserve it. What bad thought did we think?
What bad deed did we do? We all are vulnerable to
these thoughts, for we all think and do things of which we
are ashamed. Is there anyone here today who could
claim otherwise? We all think and do things of which we
are ashamed. And sometimes those things do have consequences. They do cause or help to cause bad things to
happen.

The leap we dare not make, however, is to decide that
God has willed or allowed this bad thing to happen
because of our bad thought or deed. Think about it: if
God's desire that good things happen was dependent
upon us being good, how could anything good come
about? If God's desire for us to be healthy were dependent upon our never doing anything bad for our bodies,
who of us could be healthy? If God's love for us was
dependent upon whether or not we feel lovable, we all
would be lost.

The radical claim of the gospel is that God's love is not
dependent upon our fleeting feelings. God's desire for the
good and beautiful is not dependent upon whether or not
we deserve the good and the beautiful. God is bigger
and better than that. God is able to love even those we
do not, cannot, love. And there is a bigger miracle than
that: God is able to love us, even when we do not love
ourselves. God wants what is beautiful and best for us
even when we don't deserve it.

Now, I am not trying to argue that only good things
happen, or that somehow everything that happens is really for the good. That is ridiculous and you who have
suffered know it. Here is what I claim: that evil and suffering are not the consequence of the will of God. Your
tears and pain are not what God wants.

Scripture says that God created the world amidst

chaos—and the chaos keeps breaking back into creation to cause havoc. God took a great chance with this beautiful creation that surrounds us. Chaos is dangerous. It can destroy the created. But creation itself is creative. And creativity can be used to build up beauty or to destroy it. We take this same chance everytime we create. That which we create is at risk. Something or someone could come along and destroy or damage it. The creation itself could cause suffering of others. This is true of our most beautiful

God does not actively will evil and suffering. But God is present with us in evil and suffering, including the evil and suffering of HIV/AIDS.

works of art and music. Art or song designed to bring truth and beauty can also bring wrenching tears. This is true of children. Children we decide to bring into the world to share in life's joy will also share in life's sorrow. It is true even of friendship. The friendships we create will bring great joy, but only at the risk of causing real pain from time to time.

This is the nature of being creative amidst the chaos of the world. God didn't design the chaos any more than we did. The chaos is what is. The miracle is that the good and the beautiful can happen even in the midst of it. So here, in the midst of chaos, is God who loves you and seeks to protect you. Here amidst the chaos is a God who hovers over your life as a mother eagle hovers over her nest. Just like that mother eagle, God loves and hopes to protect you, not because of anything you can do to earn that love, but because you are God's own creation, and God adores you just as you are.

Now God also adores all of the creative possibilities in you. God loves the you that can be and is not yet. God wants you to live well and beautifully. God wants you to respect yourself and others, and to make a difference in this world. This means that there is no need for shame or self-destructive habits. If these have been a part of your past, they need not be a part of your future. Amidst our shame, we have sometimes believed that we are destined forever to stumble along in clumsy, pedestrian lives. But God wants us to fly—to soar with wings like an eagle. And when we venture from the nest, and if our wings fail to hold us aloft, God, just like that mother eagle, seeks to swoop beneath us, and bear us up. Does this mean that God can protect us from all risk? Not yet. The chaos of the world continues to break in. Evil is still alive and well. But the kingdom is coming. Patiently and inexorably, God's creativity is bringing about a reign of love. Love will rule—even in the most unlovely of hearts.

Chapter Four

Preaching as a Source of Knowledge

John Calvin highlights the importance of knowledge in the Christian community. "Nearly all the wisdom we possess, that is to say, true and sound wisdom, consists of two parts: the knowledge of God and of ourselves."[1] As sources of true and sound wisdom, most Christians today want to ensure that nature and social awareness are included in the sources of wisdom. Most contemporary Christian communities agree that one of the goals of preaching is to contribute to the congregation's knowledge of God so that the congregation can perceive God's purposes and can respond adequately in the full spectrum of personal and corporate life.

If increase in knowledge is a goal of preaching, the question immediately comes up, What does it mean "to know"? What can the pastor expect to take place in the minds and hearts of the congregation as a result of hearing a sermon? How can the sermon lead to the increase of the knowledge of God, self, and world?

These questions are vital as the preacher contemplates the nature of authority, truth, and modes of discourse. These issues are so important that philosophers and theologians often speak of epistemology (a philosophical term that refers to reflection on what and how we know) as one of the leading questions of philosophy.

Knowledge in the Premodern and Modern Eras

Discussion about knowledge has been central to the Western philosophical tradition since Socrates.[2] Plato framed the most common philosophical position: Knowledge is the accurate apprehension of the relationship between appearance and reality. Many people who lived outside the range of philosophical discussion operated with a similar understanding of knowledge. In a village, to know was to be initiated into the community's myths and mores.

In premodern culture, knowledge often has a relational dimension. Knowledge is more than the consciousness of the components that make up reality. It is also the awareness of one's relationship to reality and its particular parts. In many premodern communities, knowledge is a function of the whole self; knowledge is the integration of conscious thought, emotional response, and behavior. A key test of the accuracy of the knowledge of a person or community is the life that issues from its thought and feelings. For instance, Isaiah says, "The ox knows its owner, and the donkey its master's crib; but Israel does not know, my people do not understand" (Isa. 1:3).[3]

The premodern preacher sought to help the congregation have proper information about (and relationship with) God and the world. For example, in this respect, Calvin's editor comments, "Knowledge . . . is for Calvin never 'mere' or 'simple' or purely objective knowledge. . . . Probably 'existential apprehension' is the nearest equivalent in contemporary parlance."[4]

In the modern world, knowledge was regarded as the conscious possession of "bricks" of reliable information.

The empiricists equated knowledge with mastery of factual data gathered through the five senses. Researchers sought to suspend their biases and perceptions as they searched for objective facts. Moderns thought of knowledge as the possession and control of "bricks" of information.[5] Science, with its empirical method, became the epitome of knowledge. Modern people understood education as the accumulation of such bricks.

Progress came to be associated with technological expansion, and the scientist became the high priest of progress. Many human beings believed that they would continuously improve their quality of life in the world by accumulating enough data and manipulating it technologically, or by improving its processes.

The rationalists identified reason as the source of knowledge. In the rationalist paradigm, knowledge is that which coheres with the necessary principles. Rationalism did not become as influential in the modern popular consciousness as empiricism. Nonetheless, the rationalists joined with others in modernity to leave a legacy of popular concern for consistency. Many modern people, who have never heard of Descartes, value logical coherence and aim to eliminate contradiction from their intellectual visions and their lifestyles.

Both the empiricists and rationalists were sympathetic to the concerns of the other. The empiricists honored the reasoning of the rationalists. That which could be proven true by means of experience ought logically be true in every situation. The empiricists aimed for knowledge that was universally coherent. And the rationalists sought to take account of actual experience.

Both the empiricists and the rationalists regarded knowledge as primarily a function of the conscious mind. Many modern people mistrusted feeling and other nonrational experiences or awarenesses as sources of knowledge. Feeling could not be described with scientific precision or verified empirically. Nor did feelings follow the logic that was necessary for a rationalistic understanding of knowledge.[6]

The modern preacher wanted the congregation to be confident of what it could know (and what it could not know) about the Bible, God, Jesus Christ, the Holy Spirit (and other foci of Christian belief). To oversimplify, we might say that as the modern era developed, preaching unfolded along two lines.

One group of preachers who were under the sway of empiricism or rationalism tended to strip away those elements of the Bible and Christian conviction that could not pass scientific or logical muster. They sought to help the congregation identify a core of beliefs that could stand the tests of modernity. Other preachers reacted against these emphases and sought to show that modern conceptions themselves provided a basis for adhering to traditional views of the Bible and other matters of Christian faith. Thus, a sermon on "Why I Preach That the Bible Is Literally True" might rely upon the modern notion that the facts recorded in the Bible can be demonstrated to be empirically and logically true.

The modern world fragmented knowledge into separated categories, such as science, mathematics, psychology, philosophy, religion. A culture of specialists came about. While the specialists have great expertise within their specialty, they are frequently isolated and unable (or unwilling) to talk seriously with those outside their specialty. The results have been disastrous for religion. Religion has become only one brick of knowledge alongside others, and seldom interacts with them.

The modern sermon was designed to speak to conscious understanding. If a change in thinking or acting were desired, the preacher would show, empirically and (or) logically, why the congregation should adopt the change. The sermon appealed to reason as the basis for life perception and action. Stories and images were important because they illustrated (or otherwise helped the congregation grasp) the major (cerebral) point.

Many postmoderns see limitations in modern views of knowledge. As noted earlier, the modern notions presuppose a universality of knowledge that does not take account of the particular contexts within which individuals and communities know. Human beings cannot achieve the interpretation-free state required for scientific observation. Science is constantly revising (even contradicting) many of its own "conclusions." Postmodern communities increasingly recognize that scientific and technological developments can be destructive; the noncritical use of science and technology inflames some of our world's present problems (especially with respect to the environment and possibilities for war). The division (and subdivision) of knowledge into specialties has led to the "fragmentation of knowledge." Representatives of the different realms of knowledge have difficulty interacting with one another; the various disciplines sometimes see themselves in competition.

The separation of science and religion has been especially unfortunate. This disjunction has left science without values to inform its directions or conclusions. "The physicist or the biologist is accountable to no one other than the lords of their own subjects."[7] And the knowledge of religion often seems irrelevant to the scientifically minded. Many postmodern communities are increasingly aware that knowledge is more than the possession of facts. One of the modern educational fallacies is that increasing amounts of reliable information (data) will inevitably lead to better persons and a better world.

Knowledge in the Postmodern Ethos

Many postmodern people view knowledge in ways that continue the modern world's desire for incisive awareness, while recovering the premodern community's transrational, relational notion of knowledge. However, the two cannot be simply (and romantically) pasted together, but must be tempered and filled out with postmodern recognitions.

The drive for precision in knowledge is an irreversible gain of modernity. In the physical and social sciences, a postmodern inclination is to describe objects, events, persons, communities, and the natural world as fully as we can. In the realms of values, ethics, and religion, postmodern people often state as clearly as they can what they believe and what they do not. These descriptions help postmodern people make their way through contemporary life. For instance, on what can we really count from God when we pray?

In the postmodern ethos, people seek knowledge that integrates as much factual understanding as is possible with depth of intuition and feeling.

At the same time, postmodern constructs lead us to be aware of the contingency of such knowledge. We often perceive only that which our worldviews or categories or socialization have prepared us to notice. Today's breakthrough may be tomorrow's castoff. A change in perspective may lead us to regard today's trash dump as the seedbed for tomorrow's future. I often discover that I thought I knew in full when I knew only in part.

Furthermore, many postmodern communities think of human understanding as a full fabric that interweaves hard data, the capacity to reason, and emotion. Susanne K. Langer describes this expanded realm of understanding as feeling. While feeling includes emotion, it is much more. "The word 'feeling' must be taken here in its broadest sense, meaning everything that can be felt, from physical sensation, pain and comfort, excitement and response, to the most complex emotions, intellectual tensions or the steady feeling-tones of a conscious human life."[8] Knowledge is a function of the human gestalt. "We think with our bodies."[9] Such knowledge cannot always be described with arithmetic accuracy. Indeed, Bernard Meland notes, "We live more deeply than we can think."[10] Whitehead muses, "Mothers can ponder many things in their heart which their lips cannot express."[11] Much of our knowledge is tacit. As Michael Polanyi explains, "We can know more than we can tell."[12]

Poets, musicians, sculptors, playwrights, and others of sensitive spirit can frequently express the knowledge of feeling through **As Whitehead notes, we think with our bodies.** artistic media. However, the arts cannot always capture the depths and complexities of tacit knowledge. We know some things simply in the act of knowing.

This amplified notion is particularly important when speaking about the knowledge of God. God is not available for empirical analysis in the same way that a scientist can examine a chemical compound. However, the congregation can be aware of many of the effects of God's presence in the world. The preacher can help the community recognize these apprehensions of the divine that come to the congregation in its wholistic experience. The congregation can *feel* God's presence.

The preacher seeks for the congregation to recognize correspondence between the sermon's claims about God and the congregation's depths of experience. A significant part of the preacher's calling is to help the congregation *name* the divine presence in the world (and to help the congregation make a suitable response).

For instance, a basic Christian affirmation is that God is with each and ever member of the congregation (and is with each and every member of the human race, and indeed, is with each and every created entity from the tiniest particle to the biggest and most far-off galaxy) each and every moment of each and every day. The preacher can help the congregation increase (or reaffirm or enlarge) its knowledge of this reality by helping the congregation correlate the claim with its experience. The preacher can encourage the congregation to become cognizant of (and to respond to) feelings and awarenesses that may be prompted by the divine presence.

In order to know the divine purpose in a particular situation, the preacher needs to have criteria by which to identify the divine presence and its leading in the world. I develop three such criteria in the next chapter.

Four Ways the Sermon Can Increase the Congregation's Knowledge

If human understanding is a gestalt, I should not speak of four "ways" in which sermons can increase the congregation's knowledge. But for heuristic purposes, I allow myself the oversimplification of speaking in this fashion, recognizing that these different notions are vitally interrelated.

First, the sermon can bring basic information concerning Christian faith to the congregation. Some postmodern preachers rightly point out that knowledge is more than information. Furthermore, God's grace, not information, is salvific. However, Christians need some basic information in order to move toward optimum Christian functioning. Christians should know the generative stories of the Bible (and how to interpret them), as well as foundational Christian doctrines and ethical principles, and how to apply those principles in today's world. From my perspective, Christians need to know how to engage in the mutual critical correlation of Christian tradition with contemporary life.

The sermon can help the congregation develop knowledge in four ways: (1) Providing basic information about the Christian tradition; (2) Naming experience that correlates with Christian understanding; (3) Correcting misperceptions; (4) Speaking to the life of feeling.

In an earlier time, a pastor could assume that the congregation was familiar (at least at a popular level) with rudimentary Christian facts. But the pastor in the postmodern community cannot assume that the congregation is consciously acquainted with requisite Christian information.

For instance, when the preacher says that God used the Chaldeans as instruments of the divine judgment on Israel, the listener needs to know that "Chaldeans" is another name for "Babylonians," and that the Babylonians were Israel's idolatrous enemies. If the preacher says that we are "saved by grace through faith," the congregation needs to know what it means to be saved, how grace effects salvation, and how faith is related to grace and salvation.

Second, the preacher can help the congregation name aspects of their general experience in Christian terms. In the last fifty years, much literature in Christian education has emphasized that most people have life experiences, perspectives, feelings that correlate with dimensions of Christian faith. However, they do not often have a framework of understanding or Christian language by which to relate much of this unnamed material to Christian comprehension. For instance, members of the listening community have experiences of unconditional love or sin without realizing the theological dimensions of these realities. The preacher can help the congregation recognize the divine activity and call in such experiences.

The theological grounding of this notion is quite simple. God is omnipresent. Since God seeks for all to know God's unconditional love and to respond with justice, God is ever active in every life to help these qualities come to expression. Therefore, people have experiences of God's love and will for justice even when they cannot explain them as such. Aidan Kavanaugh notes that the preacher's calling is then not always so much to "instruct the unknowing in the Unknown" as it is to "trigger the myriad awarenesses of that same absolute reality all members of the group bring with them."[13]

For example, if the sermon centers on God's grace, the preacher might define grace, and explain that grace is God's unmerited favor toward us and all. The preacher could assure the congregation that they already stand in God's grace. The preacher might then help the congregation remember their experiences of unmerited favor that are analogous to the experience of God's grace. The preacher might then help the community recognize moments in its life when divine grace has been particularly manifest. The sermon could encourage the people to recognize other moments when God's grace is noticeable. The sermon could lead people to respond to the knowledge of grace.

Along the way, the preacher needs to help the congregation formulate criteria by which to judge the degree to which ideas, events, experiences, and feelings respond to the presence of God, or the degree to which they frustrate God's purposes.

Third, the preacher may need to help the congregation correct some of its views of Christian faith. Members in the community may need to replace old and unreliable knowledge with fresh and more adequate perspectives. For the last couple of generations, the lack of vibrant teaching ministry in the long-established denominations has left many Christians with anemic faith perspectives. Persons in the church, and in the wider culture, sometimes mistake civil religion, elements of New Age spirituality, or the views of media talk shows for the Christian message. The preacher must sometimes call the congregation to see the disparities between their current misperceptions and the convictions of more mature Christianity.

Fourth, sermons ought to speak to the full range of the congregation's knowledge. Of course, sermons should provide basic factual data about the subject of the sermon. And they ought to contain clear ideas that the congregation can understand and relate to their everyday lives. In addition, sermons should touch the life of feeling. Much, perhaps most, of human understanding takes place at the level of feeling.

How does the sermon connect with the feeling of the congregation? Many ideas *qua* ideas energize the total self. I have felt electricity run through my body when significant thoughts have come onto the screen of my mind's computer. Beyond ideas, Fred Craddock long ago noticed that stories and images have unusual power to penetrate the deepest recesses of human knowledge. The preacher seeks to help the congregation develop images out of which to understand God and the world.

Toward this end the preacher needs to remember that images are replaced "quite slowly." The congregation may say an intellectual yes to a preacher's concept. They may agree to replace an old idea with a new one, but frequently images associated with the old continue to hang in the congregation's heart. The image itself and its web of feeling associations need to be replaced. Until then, the congregation is torn; it may be doing battle with itself "and possibly making casualties of itself in the process. This change takes time because the longest trip a person takes is from the head to the heart."[14]

Many in contemporary homiletics suggest that the sermon itself can be an experience through which the congregation enters into larger or more focused worlds. Here is a guiding question for the preacher in the postmodern setting who desires to integrate the yearning for precise thinking with the life of feeling: *What experience does the sermon seek to evoke or create in the listener?*[15]

Each sermon calls for a different purpose, and, consequently, a different level of emphasis on factual data, clear ideas, feeling. The purpose for the sermon comes into focus as the preacher meditates on the congregation's needs in the light of the norms and resources of the gospel. One sermon may aim to add to the congregation's factual knowledge base or its feeling associations with a given theological concept. Another might want to help correct the congregation's behavior. Still another sermon might want to help the congregation put its good behavior under proper theological management. A sermon might lead the congregation to reject some of its cherished values and practices and replace them with others. Some sermons could be designed to help the congregation name what is already present but unrecognized in the congregation's heart, in its community life, or in its larger social setting. Whatever the purpose of the particular sermon, the preacher ultimately hopes that it will mediate the full knowledge of God.

A Perspective from Scott Black Johnston

For now we see in a mirror, dimly, but then we will see face to face. Now I know only in part; then I will know, fully even as I have been fully known.   *(1 Cor. 13:12)*

The Limits of Knowledge

The faithful preacher is in constant pursuit of knowledge. Each week, pastors are faced with changing, critical questions to which they must seek informed, theological answers. What is this biblical text saying? What is happening in the world? Who are the community of the faithful? What is God's word for this day? These investigations are the bread and butter of the preacher's life. With a fervor befitting our calling, we chase after accurate answers and search for authoritative knowledge; all so that we might shape clear words about God in uncertain times.

In recent years, however, the work of postmodern thinkers suggests that we may actually be hunting for a specter that cannot be caught. Knowledge, these scholars tell us, is rather elusive prey.

Why are postmodern scholars skeptical when it comes to our ability to seek and obtain knowledge? To begin an answer, we need to consider modernity. As a period of human history, modernity may be best characterized as a time of optimistic trust in our ability to gain knowledge and to conquer uncertainty. It was possible, we thought, to know everything about the inner workings of the atom, to be sure about the base principles of mathematics, and to discern an irrefutable system of fundamental logic. With such positivism as a driving force, the projects of modernity worked to uncover what they considered to be the very foundations of science.

Today, however, as postmodern thinkers look back on the achievements espoused by modernity, they point out that these philosophers and scientists did not dig as deeply (i.e., uncover the bedrock of knowledge) as they once thought. The atom has proved much more complex than originally proposed. Mathematics appears no closer to a confirmed, rational foundation, and everybody seems to have a different definition of "logic." Indeed, the shortfalls of modernity have led many contemporary thinkers to suggest that the time for intellectual optimism is past. For it is impossible to identify certain, essential foundations for our intellectual endeavors. Knowledge, the postmodernists argue, has its limits.

Postmodern thinkers expose the limitations of knowledge. All human knowing is cast in a provisional light.

Perhaps the limits of our ability to know something with certainty can be felt most poignantly when we study our basic concepts. Take, for example, the word *justice*. What does justice mean? For the postmodern scholar, it is no longer feasible to suggest that there is a universal concept in existence somewhere that can be described by the word *justice*. Instead, justice is understood differently by different groups of people who define the term. So, to some people, justice means food for the poor, while to others, there is only justice when people get what they deserve. To one group, justice means the ability to shoot back, while to another group justice refers to passive resistance in the face of violence. To some, justice refers to God's righteous judgment. To others, it means a "not-guilty" verdict in a criminal court. In a world in which we have no access to the essential meaning of justice, we quickly find ourselves faced with innumerable competing definitions for the term. Unable to locate a foundation that can provide a universal description of critical concepts such as justice, all knowledge is pronounced "provisional" in the postmodern world. Consequently, the definitions of our most crucial terms (such as God, freedom, gender) have become disputed territory on the postmodern battleground. What are the implications of this struggle for the contemporary preacher?

The Carnival of Meaning

Clearly, the provisional nature of human knowledge is not confined to the secular world. As postmodern a/theologian Mark C. Taylor points out, theological concepts also lack firm definitions. Our cherished words about God, Taylor writes, are really part of a huge, intricate web in which concepts, words and contexts change as they "condition and mutually define each other."[16] According to Taylor, the constantly varying character of our theological terms makes it neither desirable nor possible to attribute the meaning of our words to a firm foundation.[17] Therefore, argues Taylor, it is time to develop a new theological model that can take account of the capricious quality of our words.[18]

To that end, Taylor claims that theology is best understood as "erring." "To err is to ramble, roam, stray [and] wander."[19] Theology as erring is an act of serpentine playfulness. The erring theologian pulls apart words—revealing and reveling in their multiple meanings. Taylor delights, for example, in the notion of "mazing grace."[20] Since God is dead, according to Taylor, we have lost grace. Yet, in a "delirious and deluded sense," he claims, we can realize *mazing grace* through the free play of a/theology. *Mazing grace* is a description of our labyrinthine condition—we wander through an endless cavern where words have no foundations and we have no possibility of escape.[21] We live in the "absence of center and logos, [where] there is no special time or special place."[22] This is the description of the postmodern condition that Taylor would have us embrace. To do so, theology must become an act of comedy, a carnival, an instance of frivolous play that erases every center for knowledge while dancing above a bottomless abyss.

Are preachers in the postmodern context constrained to follow Taylor's path? Should we abandon the search for knowledge, forsake theological inquiry into biblical texts and congregational lives, and give ourselves over to capricious uncertainties? If, as Taylor writes, "when certainty is unattainable, everything remains undecidable," then is all knowledge of God impossible?[23]

Full Knowledge

Clearly, Taylor is justified in pointing out the changing nature of theological terms and concepts. He

We cannot have full knowledge of God.

101

is also correct to remind us of the uncertainty that is inherent in any attempt that we make to know God, self, other, or history. We never have a complete, sure, or untainted knowledge of any concept or person, nor do we have such knowledge of God. So, when Ron states in his concluding comments on knowledge, that the purpose of preaching is "to mediate the full knowledge of God," I find myself disagreeing. While "full" knowledge seems a laudable goal—Moses on Mt. Sinai sought such access to the divine (Exodus 33)—it does not seem to be something that humans are in a position either to communicate or understand. We must remember that Moses, with his face pressed firmly into a mountain crevice by the hand of the Almighty, was able to catch only a reflected glint of God's passing glory. Indeed, Moses is protected from having a more direct encounter with his Creator, for as God informs him, full access to the face of the divine would surely prove fatal. Preachers should detect a note of caution in this ancient theophany. Attempts to convey the fullness of God in our sermons are ultimately futile and actually undesirable; for full knowledge of the divine is something that finite beings are neither able to convey nor equipped to handle.

Real Presence

Yet, if "full" knowledge is both unattainable and undesirable, is there still something left for preachers to pursue? Was Moses able to discern anything from his position in the crevice? Both of these questions should be answered with a yes. For it is not at all clear, once we have recognized that uncertainty inheres in our vocabulary, our systems and our experience, that the end result of this realization will be the unraveling of all knowledge and the failure of communication.

Taylor points out that theology concerns itself with questions of "presence." How is God present to God's self? How is God present to us in the text of the Bible, in history, and in the Lord's Supper? Modern philosophy concerns itself with similar questions. How can humans make themselves present to each other? According to Taylor, each time we attempt to encounter the presence of God in a text or in history, or even as we try to make ourselves present to another human being through our words, the fragmented nature of our signs leads to failure. Ultimately, the only thing that is present to the postmodern theologian is *absence*—absence of self, other, text, and most important, God.[24] This is a peculiar argument; for by asserting that without full presence, there must be absence, Taylor "gives in" to a reductionistic bipolarity, something that he earlier criticizes.[25] Must there be an either/or in terms of presence and absence? When "full" presence is impossible, is absence the only remaining option?

Throughout history, theology has displayed considerable nuance in relation to the presence and absence of God. Realizing that God's full presence is an eschatological hope, theologians have long confessed that we live in the "now and not yet." Accordingly, we have come to understand that "absence" and "presence" are not simple conceptual opposites. In the Lord's Supper, for example, many Christians refuse to collapse "presence" and "absence" by asserting the *real* (rather than *full*) sacramental presence of Christ. Centuries ago, Calvin articulated this position, stating that in the Supper, "the whole Christ is present, but not in his wholeness"; and faithful communities continue to live in and through this dialectical mystery, hanging on to mediated, uncertain and often unclear revelations for the real presence that they convey even in the midst of absence, even as we wait for the full presence of the one to come.[26] The *all* or *nothing* understanding of presence that lies at the root of Taylor's project reveals a postmodern theorist who is surprisingly uncomfortable living in the in-between times.

Uncertain Revelations

We cannot, as Ron claims, have "full knowledge" at this time. Yet, we must not despair, for preachers are called to pursue sufficient knowledge of God—knowledge that will sustain the faithful even as we await the eschaton and the full revelation of the divine.

As the apostle Paul writes in 1 Corinthians, we live in that time when full knowledge does not lie within our grasp—we "know only in part." That must be sufficient. For, God still calls preachers to study diligently and to speak knowledgeably. Both Ron and Barbara remind us of this in this chapter on knowledge. Barbara turns to the scriptures to develop a complex understanding of "justice." Ron reminds us that Christian language gives us a framework to understand God in the world.

While none of us has said all there is to be said about knowledge, each of us has attempted to utter some true words on the subject. This is fitting. For the focus of the preacher's efforts should be on what it means to know and speak of God *truly*, rather than to know and mediate God *fully*.[27]

As preachers, then, we exist in the bind between seeing through a clouded glass and being called to report on our limited viewings. As witnesses to the truth of Christ, we can neither refrain from straining our theological eyes to discern what it is that we are called to preach, nor can we forget that the words that we use to proclaim God's reign are provisional. Once again, this is our affliction, and it reminds us that we only know God to the extent that God acts to be revealed. As Barth puts it:

We can and must act as those who know. But we must not claim to be those who know. For if our knowledge of this fact from its self-revelation is not new every morning, if it is not newly received from it, with empty hands, as a new gift, it is not this knowledge at all . . . Its power consists in the divine act of majesty in the face of which those who really know will always find and confess that they do not know. The attitude of those who know in this power can only be one of greatest humility.[28]

Our calling is to exist between the absence and presence of full knowledge, to have only a limited vantage point (perhaps pressed into the side of a mountain), and yet, from that place to articulate a word which, given divine grace, might allow listeners sidelong, incomplete, yet true glimpses of the living God.

A Perspective from Barbara Blaisdell

Knowledge is justified true belief. I recognize that this is a thoroughly modern formulation. But I believe it to be accurate. It requires that I take responsibility for what I believe to be true—that it be justified by experience and moral intuition. It requires conversation with others to test the processes of justification that I have used. In other words, it asks if my process of justification is also adequate to account for the claims to knowledge that others make about their experiences. If not, I may well hold a belief that is not true (or, perhaps, the other person holds such a belief), and further conversation and mutual assessment is required. This means, as Ron has written, that knowledge is more than information.

But even knowledge, so construed, is not enough for the postmodern who would preach: for the postmodern preacher, "knowledge" must seek its way toward wisdom. Wisdom is more

Christian knowledge requires more than correct information integrated with feelings that are congruent

105

with the gospel. Christian knowledge is not complete until it becomes wisdom.

than feeling. It is a depth of understanding beyond surface rationality or mere passion. Wisdom is a profound uniting of both passion and reason. For a sermon to communicate this kind of depth, it must lead the listeners in a dance of reason and passion, thought and feeling. It will not deny knowledge as information, but it will seek to fulfill knowledge in wisdom and understanding.

In an excerpt from a sermon on Jesus' encounter with Zacchaeus, Barbara illustrates the struggle to go beyond Christian information about grace and justice toward Christian wisdom in understanding the complicated relationship between these matters. How does God's grace call us to relate to persons at whom we are passionately (and rightly) outraged because of their practice of injustice?

Allow me to illustrate, from my own preaching, one of the challenges of a spiritual life: that of coming to a reasonable understanding of the gospel's dual claims of justice and grace, and a depth awareness of the complexity of those claims as they affect one's own inner life. Justice cannot exist without passionate outrage at injustice. Yet, passionate outrage is the enemy of grace. Jesus turns to this theme over and over again, asserting the demand of God for justice, framing that demand with grace. Often our preaching focuses on grace one Sunday, judgment the next, never addressing the depth of complexity with which the two themes interact in actual experience.[29]

Consider that moment in Jesus' life (Luke 19:1-10), when he is standing underneath a tree, looking up into its branches. He is surrounded by a crowd of people who also are looking up into those branches. If you were to walk up on such a scene, wouldn't you want to know what was in that tree?

So we look up ourselves, and through the leaves, we see a little man. He doesn't look like a very nice little man. (Paul Duke says if we were filming this story today, we'd cast Danny DeVito in this part.) Picture Zacchaeus—in the body of Danny DeVito—with his leering smile and licentious laugh. And all those people in the crowd around you will be happy to tell you that this man is a traitor. He takes money from his own people and hands it over to foreign occupiers. What's more, he's a thief. These are poor people. And Zacchaeus charges them more than what they owe and lines his own pockets with the surplus. God only knows what else he's done. Wealthy politicians are often caught up with countless other vices.

We have taught our children in Sunday school to sing, "Zacchaeus was a wee little man, and a wee little man was he." I suspect that people in Jericho would more likely be singing, "Zacchaeus is a slimy little snake, and a scuzzy little creep is he."

The congregation knows that it ought to be outraged when Jesus invites Zacchaeus to dinner. Zacchaeus is a crook.

Now, the crowd turns to Jesus, the holy one, the famous ethics teacher who has just arrived in this town, and in the very first moments of his visit he stops at this tree and peers up at the diminutive little crook perched on a limb with a view. Jesus squints up at him for a while. The crowd waits. Everybody waits. And then to everyone's astonishment, Jesus says, "Zacchaeus, hurry down. I'm doing lunch at your house today."

This was not a crowd-pleasing speech. Nobody was smiling at this idea. Even Jesus' colleagues didn't smile. They all gasped! It is fashionable for the preacher at this point in the story to chastise the crowd for self-righteousness. But this undercuts the radicality of the gospel claim of grace. Zacchaeus is not a nice man. The crowd ought to be outraged as well. Imagine if you will, your savior Jesus Christ sitting down at table right in front of you and your clergy colleague found guilty of sexual misconduct . . . or the young dealer who tried to sell drugs to your kid last week. What is Jesus thinking? Now, we've read ahead in the text and we know that Zacchaeus reforms, but at the time of this lunch date, and in the full knowledge of the entire crowd, Jesus is pledging conversation to a selfish, unrepentant little crook. It surely isn't who we expect Jesus to keep company with.

What's worse, Jesus continues to keep such company, and we continue to be outraged by it. We are more than startled when we run into these people in the church. Is there a pastor who has not been hurt by the church? Hurt trivially or hurt profoundly by the very people who have the love of God on their lips? It is wrong. It shocks and dismays us. How can this person be called a Christian? Or perhaps, in a wonderful idealistic fervor, you committed yourself to helping someone in need, only to discover that the needy person is not grateful, not deserving, not honest. And so you wonder, why bother?

The church is not always safe. And church work—doing justice and showing mercy—is certainly not safe. We wish it could be. We think it should be. But in the end it can't be. Because Jesus keeps inviting himself to lunch with dangerous people. And Jesus keeps insisting that we, too, break bread with dangerous people. This is the gospel claim of grace—and it hooks our valid outrage at injustice.

Because of the lavishness of God's grace, the church is not safe. Jesus calls us to break bread with dangerous people.

So why bother? If we cannot ensure that the church will always be loving, if we are not always safe even here, why bother? Well, finally, you and I are not here because of each other. Ultimately, we are not here because of the saints (and sinners) past and present

Clergy are in the ministry because Jesus has stood beneath us and called.

who make up the church. In the end, you and I are in this ministry because Jesus has come and stood beneath us. When we have placed ourselves on a high and mighty perch of self-righteous anger or of self-satisfied arrogance, when we have climbed high into the branches of self-destruction or self-pity, Jesus has come to stand beneath us, calling us by name, and said gently: Come down from there. I want to break bread with you this morning. When we have been most ill-tempered or bigoted, most bitter and angry, when we have belittled ourselves with our sins, when we have been slimy little worms and scuzzy little creeps, Jesus has come and called out our name and bids us, "Come up here and break bread with me."

This is our story of the gospel. But I hope it is not mere storytelling. Depth of knowledge demands hard reason. Grace is a hard reality, not a pleasant sentiment. Its intention is not to soften the claims on our lives to do justice. It intends to reveal to our deepest selves the knowledge of our own inadequacies, our inability to save ourselves. Without the grace of God and conversation with the community, we often cannot even see the differences between justice and injustice.

The sermon that intends to communicate wise knowledge, deep knowledge, will offer an experience of the dance of passionate reason and reasoned passion. It will be justified; that is, authentic to the full range of experience and intuition of the preacher. It will be tested for truth by an appreciative awareness of the experience of others. Not just any others will do. Allegiance to truth-seeking in the postmodern era

At its best, Christian preaching is a dance of passionate reason and reasoned passion. demands that we share the experiential table with those whose perspectives are radically other than our own. To be postmodern, we must do this. But, on the other hand, we will not be Christian in that encounter if we simply substitute such a conversation (and the discomfort it may cause) for claims to truth. Notice that Jesus did not say to Zacchaeus, "Whatever is true of your experience is okay for you." That would have been a lie, and inappropriate to the gospel. Thus, a sermon authentic to the preacher and tested by the experience of others must also be tested for appropriateness to the gospel—the dual universal claims of God's unconditional love for all and God's will for justice for all.

Chapter Five

Preaching About God in a Postmodern Setting

A Perspective from Ronald Allen

The call of the preacher is to speak an authoritative, truthful word from God and about God. The preacher aims to help the congregation discover (and respond to) God's presence and purposes in the world. Consequently, the preacher must have a well-considered vision of God. What is God's character? What does God offer the world? What does God ask? How does God work in the world? The answers to such questions affect directly what the preacher says about God to the congregation. The responses to such questions also affect directly what the congregation can actually expect (and cannot expect) from God, and how they act in the world. The preacher seeks a vision of God that is appropriate to Christian tradition and intelligible in the emerging postmodern ethos.

God in Earlier Worlds

In various human communities, and at diverse moments, premodern people had differing, and often complex, ideas and images of deity. The biblical tradition illustrates this complexity. Biblical literature repeatedly emphasizes the covenantal (i.e., relational) character of God. Beyond this, the Jewish people struggled with how to hold various aspects of God in tension. At times the tradition speaks of God in anthropomorphism and personification (for example, Gen. 3:8). God acts in singular events, as when God rains fire on Mount Carmel (1 Kings 18). God withdraws from the human scene and even hides (for example, Ps. 89:46).

At the same time, the tradition also knows that God transcends the ways in which God is sometimes personified or otherwise localized, or materialized. For example, the God of Deutero-Isaiah declares, "For as the heavens are higher than the earth, so are my ways higher than your ways and my thoughts than your thoughts" (Isa. 55:9). Indeed, the tradition can speak of God as omnipresent. According to Psalm 139:7-12, the writer cannot escape God's spirit, for God is present in heaven, in Sheol, at the farthest limits of the cosmos.

As the church moved into spheres that were increasingly pervaded by Greek thought, the church's theology took on a more Greek philosophical character. God was often (though not exclusively) portrayed in philosophical categories as distant, immovable, unfeeling. For example, the doctrine of the Trinity relies upon Greek constructs to come to formal expression. In postbiblical premodern preaching, sermons often sought to explain the being and activity of God. How, for instance, could the congregation understand the one-in-three of the Trinity?

The modern world brought a theological difficulty into sharp focus. How can we speak credibly of a transcendent being whom we cannot investigate empirically?

A series of related developments in the modern world combined to make it difficult for moderns to speak about God. God could not be investigated empirically. Nor could God always be shown to be a necessary first principle. The modern world developed the notion that history is that which can be objectively verified. But it was hard to correlate empirical events in the world with the movement of an invisible God. And the category of myth became enlarged in modern theology and literature. In the modern mind, myth was often tainted as the product of unenlightened, even superstitious communities.

Modernity made it difficult to believe in God. At one end

of the spectrum, some in the modern world simply gave up on God. The village atheist became a standard figure.

The deists maintained the idea of a supreme being who related to the world like a clock maker. God set the world in motion, filled it with inviolable laws to regulate nature and human society, and stepped out of the way. The preacher helped the community discover and apply these principles.

Many moderns divided the world into the realms of supernatural and natural. Through supernatural means, God would intervene in the ordinary world. But day by day, the world operated according to natural laws. This bifurcation led to a theology of "God in the gaps." The community explained all that it could on the basis of nature. When the community came to a gap in its interpretive ability, the community claimed that the action of God filled the gap.

Still other moderns "demythologize" the Bible and the Christian tradition. They hold that a biblical passage or a Christian doctrine often contains a kernel of truth about God, community, or self that is covered by a husk of mythology.

Some modern preachers interpret the supernatural element in everyday terms. For instance, I still hear preachers explain the feedings of the thousands as occasions when the people shared food that they had brought. Only last year, I heard a preacher confidently declare, "The real miracle was the sharing!" And what about Jesus walking on the water? "The boat was actually near the shore, and Jesus was only walking into the surf." In the limited visual conditions of the stormy night, he only appeared to be walking on the surface of the water.

Fundamentalist preachers argue that the Bible and the Christian tradition must be true in the modern empirical sense in order to be believable. Hence, they seek to show how the Bible (and, to a lesser degree, the larger Christian tradition) testifies to its own truthfulness. Further, they seek to show that the stories and claims of the Bible can be demonstrated to be true on the basis of empirically verifiable data (such as archaeological evidence). The fundamentalist preacher explains the meaning and trustworthiness of the Bible (and the Christian tradition), and aims for the people to respond in accordance with proven Christian claims.

At the folk level, a fair number of modern Christians (including preachers) bypass such problems by appealing to the mystery of God. When faced with a difficult problem concerning God, the Bible, Christian theology, or life, they change the subject and say, "The answer to this problem is a mystery. We cannot understand it."

The Return of the Transcendent in the Postmodern Ethos

People in the postmodern era are much more open to the possibility of the Transcendent than were many moderns. However, consistent with postmodernism's emphasis on pluralism and diversity, the church is alive with many different visions of God. Some of these visions compete with one another; a few are contradictory. Some Christians emphasize notions of God that have been central in the Bible, the creeds, or other historic sources. Others are rediscovering elements of ancient understandings of God that have been hidden in the folds of the tradition but that hold contemporary promise. Still others articulate fresh visions of God, some of them quite eclectic. Indeed, some Christians incorporate elements from other religions, and from New Age spiritualities, into their ways of understanding God.[1]

I do not have space to review and evaluate the images of God that populate the postmodern church and world. My purpose now is to commend a vision of God that is appropriate to the Christian tradition and credible in the postmodern ethos. Making use of the conceptuality of process thought, this vision is rooted in the elements of the Bible. It draws upon aspects of Christian tradition. It attempts to be sensitive to the sensibilities of contemporary people without selling out the gospel to those sensibilities. It attempts to honor the plurality and diversity of the postmodern era by showing how God relates to all creatures in all times and places, while generating a vital sense of Christian identity. This vision both partakes of the prevailing ethos and offers challenges to it. I believe that it has an authority of promise and that it is verified in the experience of believing communities today. It is a believable vision in that the congregation knows what it can—and cannot—count from God. It accounts for a broad range in the knowledge of God—informational and intuitive.

Many people in the postmodern ethos hunger for religious experience with depth and transcendence. They are receptive to the preacher's message. In this situation, the preacher must be careful to represent God in ways that are continuous with Christian tradition and genuinely credible to contemporary sensitivities. Such a message can be faithful to the gospel and can help the congregation develop a Christian identity that can withstand the lures of contemporary quick-fix spiritualities.

Schubert Ogden provides the theological clue to this vision in his frequent citation of a phrase from one of Charles Wesley's hymns to summarize the heart of this vision. Speaking to Jesus, Wesley has the congregation sing to Jesus, "Pure, unbounded love thou art."[2] For Christians, Jesus Christ reveals that God, and all of God's relationships with the world, are unreserved love. God wills love in all relationships in the world. God is intensely relational.

Building on the notions that God is love and that God wills for all creatures to live in love, my colleague Clark M.

Williamson formulates a crisp understanding of the gospel as

> the good news that God graciously and freely offers the
> divine love to each and all (oneself included) and that this
> God who loves all the creatures therefore *commands* that jus-
> tice be done to them. This dipolar gospel (a) *promises* God's
> love to each of us as the only adequate ground of our life and
> (b) *demands* justice from us toward *all* others whom God
> loves. God's justice and God's love are the two basic modes of
> expression of the one divine character, God's *hesed*.[3]

In Williamson's context, "All the creatures" include all the elements of the natural world. In this context, justice is used in its
most profound biblical sense to refer to relationships in which
all things are in accord with God's love and will. Christians
come to know the gospel through the story of Jesus Christ,
whose roots draw from the life of Israel.[4] This understanding
of the gospel derives from Christian tradition and is sympathetic to the postmodern concern for justice in community.

God is always with every created entity. I refer to this phenomenon as God's omnipresence. God is always present to
work with us to draw forth the best in every situation. God's
presence does not mean that every situation will always come
to a happy ending. But it does mean that every situation has
some possibility for divine love to be known. The divine
omnipresence also means that we never "get away" with vio-
lations of the divine love or the divine call for justice.
Although our approbations may not become public knowledge in the world, God knows them.

In the light of God's omnipresence, what sense do we
make of texts in the Bible and Christian tradition that speak
of God abandoning individuals or communities? I reply that
human beings do not always *perceive* that God is present. It
sometimes *feels* to us as though God is hiding. When dealing
with such a text, the pastor ultimately needs to try to help the

congregation see that their perception of their experience is incomplete. The preacher seeks to disclose the God who is present.

The events of the world (and in particular, the actions of human beings) make a difference to God. They do not change God's disposition, for, as Norman Pittenger says, God's "mind is unalterably and everlastingly love."[5] But the world's happenings add to (or detract from) God's own life.

These affirmations are tremendously important to the preacher and to the Christian community in these closing years of old millennium when many people and communities feel powerless. And they are especially important when the witness of the church is struggling. All that we do is important, for all that we do makes a difference (positive or negative) to God.

God never acts in a way that is hurtful of people or the realm of nature. God always acts for the good of all. To do otherwise would violate God's integrity. Such a God would never wish suffering on any living thing.

How, then, do we regard those passages in the Bible and in Christian tradition that describe God's judgment falling with painful bitterness upon individuals and communities, and upon nature? According to the vision described earlier, God cannot be the direct agent of such actions. However, the passages are still instructive. For they remind us that ideas and actions often have destructive consequences. False values and oppressive behaviors in a community create conditions that result in downfall. God does not destroy us, but we collapse under the weight of our own sin.[6]

As our discussion has revealed in earlier chapters, power and its use are important to people in the postmodern era. People are rightly suspicious of uses of power that appear to be arbitrary or abusive. Consequently, preachers need to pay careful attention to what we say about divine power.

The uses and abuses of power are important to people in the postmodern ethos. Preachers need to speak carefully and honestly of divine power. The Christian community needs to know what it can count on God to do, and what it cannot.

Emerging paradigms of God are divided with respect to the extent and use of God's power. Some Christians continue to hold that God is omnipotent in the sense of being able to do whatever God wants whenever God wants; God voluntarily chooses to restrain Godself in given situations. Others believe that God is indirectly responsible in that while God does not directly will all things, God *permits* all things. God voluntarily restrains Godself from acting. Thus, at the time of tragedy, a preacher may say, "I do not know why God allowed this to happen."

Another outlook seems to me to be especially promising for the postmodern setting. It takes a cue from the traditional problem of how to relate God's love, power, and justice. The problem is: Can God be completely loving, completely just, and completely powerful at the same time? If God has the power to end evil and suffering but does not do so, then God is not completely loving or just. God would be immoral to have such power and not to exercise it. Adherents to this view contend that God's power is limited.

God is more powerful than any other entity. Divine power is always used to lead persons and communities into just relationships. God perpetually continues working in the world to lead the world into a time when all relationships fully manifest divine purposes of love and justice.

God does not exercise power abusively. God acts by offering each person, community, and situation a higher good than its present. God seeks to lure people and nature away from evil and into more loving and just relationships. God hopes that the attractiveness of divine possibilities are such that the world's entities will respond with "Yes."

Evil results when God's partners choose not to accept the divine invitation. In this way of thinking, animals and the natural world contain their own levels of responsiveness to the divine will. A natural disaster may result from nature not affirming the divine will for love and justice.

God does not "intervene" in a situation. God does not act "supernaturally" to fill a gap. Instead, God is always present and is always working for the highest good that is available in a particular setting. As Clark M. Williamson says, "In any given situation, God is always doing everything that God can do."[7] God works with actual possibilities that are available to maximize them for the good of all. Even when persons and groups make decisions that turn against God, God continues to offer them possibilities for movement toward love and justice.

God is inexhaustible. This inexhaustibility is, to me, the mysterious quality of God. God *never* runs out of energy or capacity for imagining new possibilities for any and all situations. God is like a well that never runs dry. We human beings, accustomed to our finitude, have difficulty imagining the infinite depths of God.

Theological Criteria for Postmodern Settings

This vision of God, in concert with the postmodern context, yields three norms to evaluate any biblical text, Christian claim, idea, practice, or personal or social situation.[8]

1. *Appropriateness to the gospel.* In order to be affirmed in the Christian house, all claims, ideas, texts, values, practices, and situations should be appropriate to the gospel. That is, they should manifest God's unconditional love for each and every created entity, and they should seek for God's justice to be

The preacher in the postmodern church can employ three criteria to interpret the adequacy of any thought, feeling, or action: (1) appropriateness to the gospel; (2) intelligibility; (3) moral plausibility. These norms give the preacher a place from which to assess the differing, and often competing and contradictory, claims in the postmodern world.

known by each and every created entity. Any claim, idea, text, value, practice, or situation that denies God's love or will for justice is inappropriate to the gospel.

2. *Intelligibility.* Is a claim, idea, text, value, practice, or situation intelligible?[9] At one level, this criterion calls for logical consistency among things that Christians say and do. The church's witness ought not contradict itself. At another level, the church in the postmodern setting must be able to make sense of claims, ideas, texts, values, practices, or situations in the light of the ways in which we understand God to operate in the world, and in the light of the ways in which we understand the world itself to operate. This is an irreversible legacy of modernity.

At the same time, preacher and congregation cannot assume that their interpretations of God and the world take account of all salient factors. Preachers make the best judgments that they can, recognizing that new data or fresh perspectives may help us see things that they have not seen before.

Nor ought this criterion be used to reduce our image of God's possibilities for the world to postmodern familiarities. God transcends all of our ways of speaking about God. Postmodern perception helps us realize that the world is not a completely closed system in which all potentialities are circumscribed by natural law. God's omnipresence and inexhaustibility, in conjunction with fresh partnerships with humankind and nature, may reveal unimagined possibilities.

While new life-forms might be surprising in their details, God will always act in favor of optimum love and justice for all.

3. *Moral plausibility.* Does the claim, idea, text, value, practice, or situation call for (or demonstrate) the moral treatment of all concerned? The material or event in view of pastor and people needs to manifest love in all aspects of its behavior and action in order for it to be acceptable to Christian interpretation of reality.

An important correlate: the Bible and Christian tradition (and other sources as well) can challenge the contemporary preacher's understanding of God and of the postmodern ethos. Christian claims can ask postmodern people to reconsider significant aspects of their interpretations of the world.

These norms provide the preacher and the congregation with places to stand in the midst of diversity and relativity. However, these standards do not have imperial status. They are benchmarks by which Christians in a postmodern ethos can mark the progress of conversation about Christian faith and its implications in the postmodern setting. The norms themselves will inevitably be reformulated as our rivers of perception widen or narrow.

These criteria help preachers determine their hermeneutical relationship with claims, ideas, texts, values, practices, and situations.[10] Many biblical texts, for instance, are altogether appropriate, intelligible, and moral. For example, Hosea 11 uses a feminine image to describe God relating to the sinful community as a mother who acts for her child out of deep compassion.

A claim, idea, text, value, or practice may be expressed in language, images, and ideas that, on the surface, appear to be inappropriate, unintelligible, or immoral. But, the preacher may be able to find a positive resource for preaching by asking, "What deep point is the text intending to make? Can the sermon make a similar point in our setting? What qualifica-

Occasionally, the vision of God's gracious love and unrelenting will for justice prompts the pastor to preach against a text.

tions does the sermon need to call to the congregation's attention?"[11] For example, postmodern people may not believe the world is inhabited by suprahuman beings called demons, but the story of an exorcism may help the congregation understand God's liberating will and power.

Some texts or Christian actions are so deeply problematic that the preacher must speak against them. For instance, in Psalm 58, the author prays for God to wreak vengeance on the psalmist's enemies by breaking their teeth and causing them to "vanish like water that runs away." In the meantime, "the righteous will rejoice when they see vengeance done; they will bathe their feet in the blood of the wicked" (Ps. 58:10). To be sure, the psalm seeks to express the confidence that God will be faithful to the covenantal community.[12] But it is simply inappropriate to the gospel to pray for God to carry out such violence. However, such a text can still be an occasion for a positive encounter between the congregation and the text. For the preacher can take the text as an occasion to help the congregation reflect on the character of God and the nature and purpose of prayer.

All language about God is relative. God is above every name and form.[13] God is always more than we can envision. This fact is a trenchant criticism of all our ways of speaking of God. Like its forebears, the church in a world with postmodern tendencies is tempted to make functional idols out of our ways of speaking of God. And, ironically, some postmoderns have a tendency to absolutize the values of plurality and diversity. However, God is never without a witness in any time or place. Hence, every situation contains the potential to help us realize the overflowing abundance of the transcendent benevolence that we call God.

A Perspective from Scott Black Johnston
"Let God be God." (Karl Barth)

Firmer Ground

God is the subject of our preaching. God is the one who calls people and who bestows authority on the preacher. God is the source of divine knowledge, the giver of gospel words. God is the truth by which these words

When Christians try to speak of God, the legacy of Babel often appears to overcome the promise of Pentecost.

are measured. It is God's spirit that gathers listeners into community. It is in the name of God that we preach, baptize, and feast. Every aspect of the preaching task must seek its ground in who God is and what God requires of us.

Of course, this common starting point provides no guarantee that the Christian community will ever agree on either who God is or what God demands of us. Despite our focus on God, Christians quarrel endlessly and divisively about the character of the divine. Starting with Peter and Paul, debates have raged *disunity* since the church's inception between Jew and Gentile, Protestant and Catholic, liberal and conservative, First World and Third World, men and women, high church and low church. When it comes to discussions of God's character, we may confess that we have inherited the promise of Pentecost, but in reality we seem more in touch with the legacy of Babel.

Why so much disagreement? One way to answer this question is to return to a theme articulated in earlier chapters. Since the fullness of God is not accessible to us—since God is always shrouded to some extent in the divine mystery— then our human attempts to know God will always be limited. Consequently, one might argue that the many dis-

123

putes that Christians have had among themselves about God are a reflection of our humble status in the face of God's mysterious character.

By and large, however, such appeals to mystery have proved dissatisfying to Christians over the centuries. This is especially true in the contemporary milieu. We live in a time when competing claims about the character of God are expanding at a rapid pace. In this postmodern context, members of believing communities turn to preachers, asking the preachers to adjudicate between true and false statements about the divine. These listeners hope (and even demand) that their pastors will have more to say than "God is cloaked in mystery," or "We cannot be sure about God's character." So, now more than ever, in an effort to dispel the mists of confusion and mystery that surround God, theologians and homileticians endeavor to locate trustworthy sources of information, firm bases for faith, from which preachers can draw secure conclusions about the God we worship.

In attempting to understand who God is and what God requires of them, Christians draw on five sources: scripture, tradition, experience, reason, and community.

Christians appeal to five basic sources in order to substantiate definitive statements about the nature of God: scripture, tradition, experience, reason, and community. Clearly, these five focal points do not exist in isolation from one another. Indeed, for most believers these foundational sources intermingle in intricate ways as people endeavor to make decisions about God. Still, it is helpful to rehearse the discrete characteristics of each of these foci, for they continue to describe fundamental centers of gravity for Christians in the postmodern world. Since "reason" was addressed in chapters 3 and 4, and "community" will be considered in chapter 6, let us begin this brief survey by turning our attention to the church's primary text.

Scripture

Within the church, the Bible has long been cherished as a unique and authoritative witness to God's interactions with humankind. A great many Christians, when faced with questions regarding the character of God, endeavor to base their understanding of the divine on the biblical witness. Yet, the scope of the biblical text and the many different understandings of God that we find within it make this a persistently difficult task. For example, those seeking an answer to Christ's question, "Who do you say that I am?" will quickly find that each of the four Gospels has a distinct way of responding. In the scriptures, one encounters numerous voices engaged in many different formal acts: describing God, praying to God, challenging God, blessing and even cursing God. This literary discord makes it difficult to argue that the Bible is equipped to articulate a unified, definitive portrait of God *all on its own*. To function as a foundation, this many-voiced chorus seems to need assistance. So, to bring a sense of theological unity to the biblical text's words about God, many Christians have turned to a choir director of sorts: the tradition.

Tradition

When Christians talk about "tradition," they are most often referring to historical efforts to describe God and the life of faith in orthodox ways—in ways that are the most true. Arising out of distinctive and often volatile contexts, the creeds, catechisms, and authoritative writings of the church have attempted to unravel confused understandings of God by untangling complex strands of rationality, scripture, and experience. Those who turn to tradition as the primary foundation for making decisions about God's character find therein clear directives concerning the right ways to think and talk about God.

Of course, the tradition itself (some might say traditions) exhibits quite a bit of diversity and is often downright contradictory in making claims about the divine. Can we rely on "tradition" as a foundation for understanding God if we find it to be even more disharmonious than the Scriptures themselves? Furthermore, postmodern scholars have suggested that the conflicting elements in a tradition are evidence of the many power struggles that go on between individuals and communities—each vying to have their own particular understanding of the world verified and preserved as a benchmark for the future. If this is the case, many scholars (especially feminists) raise questions about the voices throughout Christian history that have never been heard or preserved. Can we trust a tradition knowing that it has been "corrupted" by those who would exercise descriptive power over God in order to further their own ends?

Experience

Unsatisfied with basing understandings of God on historical texts, a number of Christians, when faced with questions about the character of God, find that the most definitive guide to which they can appeal is their own experience. These people argue that the experience of living in this world is of primary importance in determining what can and cannot be said faithfully about the character of the divine.

Consider two related examples. Confronted by Nazi atrocities in World War II, a number of believers came to the conclusion that God was dead. At the same time, the experience of Elie Wiesel, a Jewish person interned in one of the death camps, led him to see God as one of the suffering. In each case, experience played a crucial role in developing an understanding of God. Of course, to rely solely on experience when making decisions about God raises the specter of relativism. Is God whatever/whomever each individual asserts? What happens when one person's experience of God and God's will impinges on another? If experience is the only foundation, then mediating between such disputes is impossible.

The Church's One Foundation

In previous chapters on truth and knowledge, Barbara, Ron, and I discussed rationality as a foundation for understanding God. From our different perspectives we found that rationality is not suitable as the sole foundation for making claims about God. In the chapter that follows, we discuss the integral role of community in the homiletical task. Even so, it will become clear that community alone cannot provide an adequate basis for making definitive statements about God.

Having examined, however briefly, each of the five sources (scripture, tradition, experience, reason, and community) to which Christians turn to provide a foundation for making determinations about the character of God, one begins to detect hairline fissures within these central sources, raising questions about the status of these sources as ultimate foundations for our talk about God. The purpose of pointing out such fissures is not finally to disparage these sources, leaving us to throw our hands up in frustration since it looks as if there is no solid basis for making determinations about God. Rather, the point is to argue that these sources (whether we appeal to them as solitary touchstones, or together like the legs of a chair) do not provide a sufficient foundation for determinative words about God.

Our search for a foundation (or even a combination of foundations) that will supersede other inadequate bases for talking about God is a sign of Christian anxiety in the face of postmodern pluralism. To the extent that this anxiety results from our desire to present a clear understanding of the gospel for the church and the world, this is a laudable neurosis. Yet, when our foundations begin to place restrictions on the free activity of God, then we have sought to ground and guarantee the truth of our proclamation in our own interpretive efforts and not in the revealing act of the divine. As Barth reminds us, "Only revelation as God's step toward us is, of course, the guarantee of its truth. As we cannot make the step across the abyss, so we cannot be the guarantee. We can only let it be guaranteed for us."[14]

Again, many will find such statements by Barth and other nonfoundational theologians to be frustrating, for they seem to lack concrete guidance. Yet, such a confession is a crucial first step in our talking about God, for it establishes the tenor for all our subsequent efforts as preachers. We are not in control of revelations. We are not masters of divinity. What we know about God, we know only because of God's activity. God (the divine subject) reveals Godself (the divine object) to human beings. If it were not for the activity of God, there would be no revelation and we would not know God.[15]

> **God is an active subject, not a passive object. Thus, the preacher who would speak about God must speak of God's actions, and the place where we most clearly see God acting is in the person of Jesus Christ.**

This situation, however, does not leave us speechless. For, the primary act of God that orients the Christian community and provides hope for the world is Jesus Christ, whose life, death, and resurrection are nothing less than God actively revealing God's character to us. This act of God, Jesus of Nazareth, is the subject of our preaching. The Christ—whom we encounter in the scriptures, whom we confess in our creeds, whom we experience in our lives, upon whom we reflect, and whom we worship in the community of believers—is the content of God's mystery. We who preach are to be humble in the face of God's mysterious and free activity, but bold in speaking of the Word become flesh.

God's Character

In his portion of this chapter, Ron develops a vision of God for the postmodern world. Within this vision, Ron identifies three criteria for evaluating biblical texts, Christian claims, and human experience in reference to God. The three criteria are (1) an understanding of the gospel based on biblical perspectives of love and justice, (2) intelligibility, and (3) moral plausibility. Ron uses this evaluative system to argue that we should preach against Psalm 58. He finds this psalm "inappropriate to the gospel" because the psalmist asks God to carry out violent acts against the psalmist's enemies. Ron's argument is compelling. For, of course, our God is not the sort who honors requests to break our enemies' teeth.

Yet, the psalm may have something more to say about the character of God. Many faithful people, faced with human atrocity, have requested that God do violence to those who engage so lustily in evil. I worry about an understanding of the gospel that rules such a prayer out of bounds. Not because I expect God to rend such evildoers limb from limb, but because I think that God can and does handle such requests. At times, the most faithful thing that we can do is to bring all that we have, and all that we are (even anger and the thirst for revenge) to God. We will not be left unchanged by such an encounter.

129

A Perspective from Barbara Blaisdell

In my contribution to chapter 3, I commented that, as a preacher, I need to explore how theology and homiletical theory play out in actual sermons. This desire reaches a particular intensity when it comes to talking about God. The preacher's words about God are the most important of all things the preacher says. For the preacher is speaking about our understanding of ultimate reality, what Scott calls "the center." Furthermore, hearers need to know concretely what God will (or can) do for them, and what God won't (or can't). Since my view of God is much the same as Ron's, I do not need to restate that presentation. I can, however, show how it shapes a specific sermon.

In the previous section, Scott raises the toughest question that can be put to any doctrine of God: the problem of evil. Scott's answer to that problem is to let God be God. Let God "handle" my prayer request to render evildoers limb from limb. To these assertions, I raise questions. What might it mean for God to "handle" my prayer request to rend evildoers limb from limb? What does it mean to let God be God? These questions, of course, raise larger questions. What is real evil? What does it look like? And what does God have to do with it?

In the face of suffering and evil, what does it mean to let God be God? What does it mean to let God "handle" my prayer request to tear evil people limb from limb?

The preacher must give a solid theological response that is both appropriate to the gospel and psychologically satisfying to Scott (and to others who have profound questions about God's role in the evil and suffering they have experienced). Let me offer again an excerpt from a sermon in which I attempt to be loyal to the church's responsibility to be appropriate to the gospel's foundation in the universal love of God and honest in the face of our individual and collective experiences of evil. The text is the parable of the wheat and the weeds (Matt. 13:24-30, 36-43). My doctrine of God allows me to say something more specific, and I think more credible and helpful, than, "Let God be God."

An example from a sermon on the problem of evil illustrates how a preacher's doctrine of God has direct implications for preaching. Preaching on the problem of evil is the "litmus test" of the adequacy of the preacher's doctrine of God.

Imagine Jesus before a crowd, on a hillside, on a fine fall day. Before him, sitting around him and down the hill are all kinds of ordinary people—old people, young people, women and men—

listening to what he has to say. And what he's been saying is something like this: "Trust the good news. The dominion of God, the kingdom of God in which God's love will rule all, is here among you, now. Don't think of it as somewhere way off in front of you in an unimaginable future. Don't think of it as somewhere lost in outer space—out there in the heavens. It is here, right here among you now!"

I cannot read the Gospel accounts of these teachings without imagining at least one person in the crowd saying, "I doubt that!" And given Jesus' character as a teacher, I hear him responding, "Good. Tell me why."

"Well, just look around you. If God's in charge in this place, it is a kingdom of corruption, not love. The empire has got its boot on our neck. Our religious leaders are corrupt. Institutional religion has done more to hurt than to help people. In the capital it's politics as usual. They're feeding off the poor. There is no justice in the land. Where is this power of God?"

Or perhaps a woman speaks up. "Last week my son died. I held him in my arms and he suffered hard. He

131

prayed. I prayed. We all prayed for his healing. But God didn't hear us. What might it mean for me to trust the good news of God's love in the here and now?"

The Gospels do not record such questions. But Matthew does record a parable that seems to indicate Jesus' response to this kind of question. Up on that hillside, in response to such questions, he must have bowed his head for a moment, and then looked up across the valley of fields and saw a farmer in the distance, harvesting. He looked at the farmers and the gardeners sitting before him and he said, "Let me tell you a story:

"Once upon a time, a farmer went to plant a field full of wheat. And he used the very best seed he could get. But on that very night, a longtime enemy of that farmer crept into the field and, by moonlight, sowed a different kind of seed. What that enemy planted, amidst the best wheat seed available, was darnel weed."

And here Jesus sees the farmers among the crowd wince. But since the city folk don't get it, Jesus pauses a minute to explain.

"Darnel weed, when it sprouts into young plants, looks just like young wheat. But it's not wheat. And it's terribly toxic. And if you eat enough of the seed, in with the wheat, it will kill you."

And now even the city folk begin to nod their heads in comprehension of the farmer's terrible problem.

"Well soon the field hands came running to the farmer and said, 'Boss, didn't you plant pure wheat seed, the very best you could get? Then how come your field is growing a crop all mixed up, weeds and wheat? Don't you want us to get busy chopping those weeds?'

"But the farmer spoke sternly, 'No. Don't touch the weeds.'"

And here Jesus notices the farmers and the gardeners frowning in confusion because no farmer in his right mind would leave the weeds alone.

"That's right," said Jesus, "that crazy farmer said to his help: Don't pull the weeds. Because," he added, "how could they know, how can you be sure which is the wheat and which are the weeds? And even if you think you're sure which is which, the roots of the weeds and the roots of the wheat are all tangled together, and you can't pull out the weeds without pulling out good wheat. And I will not risk the loss of a single stock of wheat. Let it all grow together. And then, we'll know what's what. We'll take the weeds and burn them, and we'll take the wheat to the barn."

This is not one of Jesus' more popular stories. It just doesn't rank up there with the good Samaritan and the prodigal son. In fifteen years of preaching, I've never had anyone come and ask me to talk about the one where Jesus has the farmer let the weeds take over the field of wheat. But Jesus said that's what life is like. And something in us knows it's true. The bad is all mixed up with the good. And God will not uproot the bad, for God's business is growing the good, and the good, right now, is all mixed up with the bad. The day will come when it's all sorted out. But for now, it's too soon. You and I don't live in the golden time of the final harvest. We live in the long, green, growing season where the good is stretching heavenward, growing fruitful, but whose roots are all intertwined with the bad.

Now there are questions that this parable doesn't answer in full. Why does it have to be this way? Where did the enemy come from? Why did God let him into the field in the first place? The question of the field hands is a question we'd like to put to God: "Did you, or did you not plant a good world here, God? Then

The parable does not answer all our questions about evil. Some questions must be left to another sermon. But the parable frames an essential aspect of the issue.

where did all these thorny, lethal corrupt problems come from?"

The parable just says, it is the way it is. There is God and good. And there is evil, the shadowy enemy. Both are in the world. Both have power. But this is not the world the way God dreamed it. Our disappointment with creation is God's disappointment. There are real forces of evil among us that God has not yet conquered, which means that we are stuck and God is stuck with an ambiguous world—untidy, impure, a mixed-up mess of evil and good. And God has opted not to uproot the evil, not yet. God is a strangely nonanxious farmer who will tolerate the conflict and abide the ambiguities until the growing is done.

Then the parable puts the question to us: *Can we trust such a God who will trust such a field?* Will you be patient with a God who is so patient with the evil coiled around the very root of the good? And here is what it would mean to trust and be patient with such a God: it would mean that it's not our business to sort everything out. It's not our business to wage an all-out war against the weeds, as if we could root out all the evil in the world. On this point, Jesus stood squarely against a predominant religious impulse of his time and it is a predominant religious impulse in our time: It is the "purity impulse"—which in the end is always a prideful impulse.

God is a strangely non-anxious farmer who tolerates conflicts and abides ambiguities until the growing is done. The parable raises a critical question. "Can we trust such a God who will trust such a field?"

We ought to understand where it comes from. Because all of us are *rightly* angered at the injustice and evil of this world, and for that matter all that is wrong inside us. So we want to pick up our scythes and sickles and go hacking and slashing away at the weeds of our lives and our world. Jesus forbids us to go at life this way. "You can't see," he says, "You can't see how evil and good are intertwined. And you don't see the evil you create when you judge and attack as if you were God."

Jesus does not call us to be passive when we are caught in a web of ambiguity. While we need to be patient with ambiguity, we need to root out all the evil we can.

Let's be clear, here. This story is not a call to be passive about the evils that we see. There are evils we clearly see in ourselves and in our systems that we can address and we'd better address. Christ still calls us to repentance. That means I must stop setting aside a special place in my life to cultivate weeds. I must do what I can to prevent my own sowing of evil seed. I am called to bend to the nurturing and cultivating of the good seed toward the day of harvest. But Christ warns us that the evil will not be eliminated from the fields of our lives by hacking away at it. In the struggle against evil, Christ calls us to caution and care and patience and a proper humility. Because we who think on some days that we know so much, we're part of the impure field, too. As Alvin Jackson, a preacher in the Disciples of Christ, has said, "The church is the one place where the only requirement for admittance is the acknowledgment that we don't meet the requirements for admittance." We're part of the impure field, too. There are weeds coiled around our hearts and weeds wrapped around our vision. So we don't see as clearly as we think we do. There is evil around us aplenty, and we do see it. But we do not see the damage that may come from our premature and often prideful judgments against our world and against one other.

Let me put it bluntly: We aren't here to be perfect. And we aren't here to make anybody or anything anywhere close to perfect. We are here to grow the good we can in a most imperfect field, where for now, evil and good are often wrapped up together. So for now, we are called to trust ultimate outcomes to the sovereign patience and purpose of a universally loving God. And the parable itself, as recorded in Matthew, may be God's way of handling our prayers to render our enemies limb from limb.

Individual and Community in Postmodernity

A Perspective from Ronald Allen

The relationship between the individual and the community assumes new importance for the preacher in the church in a postmodern setting. Is the sermon to speak to a collection of individuals, or is it to form a community? Or do these ways of putting the questions pose false alternatives? And what constitutes "community"? Is community comprised only of human beings? Or are animals and the natural world an integral part of a Christian vision of cosmic community? The preacher's responses to these issues have practical implications for the focus of the sermon.

Individual, Community, and Church in the Premodern and Modern Worlds

People in the premodern world understood themselves communally.[1] Scholars sometimes use the phrase "corporate personality" to describe the corporate character of human identity in the biblical world. The community is represented in the individual; the individual embodies the community. Many premodern people understand themselves to be bound indissolubly with others.[2] To be was to be a member of a community.

Premodern people had a communal vision. They understood people, animals, elements of nature, and the divine to be inherently interrelated.

Many premodern people were cosmic in their visions of

community. They often thought of the natural world as animate. The natural elements could obey God's covenantal commands to bless and curse; the natural elements could rejoice and weep.[3]

According to Genesis 1, God intends for humankind and nature to live together in mutuality. To borrow a slogan from the U.S. Army, all things in the cosmos are to work together so that each entity can be all that it was meant to be. Human beings are made in the image of God and are given dominion over nature (Gen. 1:26-28). To the premodern community, this meant that human beings are to do in our limited spheres what God does in the cosmic sphere: work toward a world in which all inhabitants and elements live together in mutuality, encouragement, and support.

Some premodern communities also believed that the cosmos was inhabited by suprahuman entities. They went by many names and functions, such as angels, mediums, demons, thrones, principalities, powers, dominions. (Some communities in the postmodern ethos—such as certain Pentecostals and New Agers—believe similarly). These agencies were a part of the cosmic community and were welcome or unwelcome according to the conditions they brought into cosmic affairs.

The preacher in this setting helps the community discover its identity and arrange its life to express that identity. The pastor helps the community develop a common memory. This memory typically includes the ancestral stories that locate the community in time, place, and meaning; it provides practical guides for everyday affairs. The preacher helps the congregation understand their individual relationships to the collective identity.

Modernity takes a turn toward individualism and anthropocentrism. Modern culture gave rise to the notion of the supreme worth of the individual who was entitled to rights.

Moderns began to think that communities were collections of individuals who were joined together by social contracts. The purpose of the larger community was to make individual fulfillment possible. Group identity did not disappear. As the many wars of the modern period indicate, such communal identity evoked loyalty.

The modern world declared that the individual human being was the supreme inhabitant of the cosmos. Everything else existed to service individuals and their quests for fulfillment.

An individual's goal in modern life was to be one's true self. Modern people thought of the individual as an independently functioning entity who achieved her or his identity. One of my high school English teachers regularly admonished us, "Be captain of your soul." These emphases intensified the drive for competition among human beings. The free enterprise system is based on the notion of competition among individuals. In the modern capitalist world, democracy becomes an ideal.

In North America, the church came into an informal partnership with the culture in which the two combined to help individuals develop into useful participants in society. The church implanted the moral consciousness that was necessary for persons to function ethically within free enterprise democracy. Many congregations and denominations became democracies that operated with the implicit assumption that the voice of the people was the voice of God. Churchly representatives often appeared in governmental and civic functions, giving the impression that the church blessed the culture.[4]

Many modern Christians conceived of the church as a collection of individuals. Sermons aimed to help individuals come to clarity about what they should (could) believe and how they should act.

Modern culture also became anthropocentric (i.e., it regarded the human being as center of the cosmos). The nonhuman inhabitants of the cosmos were here to serve the human being. Many modern people looked upon the natural realm as a collection of inanimate resources to be used by human beings in the technological development.[5] Moderns interpreted the meaning of the human being's "dominion" over nature (Gen. 1:28) to mean that the human race was free to use whatever means necessary in order to convert the raw materials of nature (including animals) into goods for human comfort and profit.

In the biblical world, salvation meant the renewal of the entire cosmos; nature itself would be redeemed. This emphasis was lost in much modern Christianity. In the modern church, salvation was often functionally reduced to the status of the relationship between the individual and God. Salvation became a matter of decision between the individual and God.

Recovery of Community Among Postmodern People

In the midst of the diversity and pluralism of the postmodern setting, many people long for community. The preacher who can show how the gospel leads to authentic community may find a receptive congregation.

Communality is a part of the vision of many postmodern people. They regard communal relationships as constitutive of human identity. They attempt to take account of the plurality and diversity of different communities. At the same time, they seek to honor the integrity of the individual and to make it possible for individuals to become all that they can.[6] Many people in the postmodern era regard the natural world as a part of cosmic community. Many postmoderns are similar to premoderns in their understanding of community. Yet, they seek to retain a high value for the individual as a part of the lasting legacy of modernity.

The most inviting statement of this worldview known to me is found in process philosophy and theology.[7] According to this thought, all human beings are internally related to other human beings, and to the natural world.[8] Human beings, and other entities, are not just objects in the same space that sometimes bump into one other. Instead, people are continually affected by other people and their circumstances in the world, and they affect us. Human beings affect, and are affected by, other entities. "Internal relatedness means that everything in some sense is *really* part of me, however dimly felt."[9] The one is included in the many; the one is more than its individuality; its participation with the many adds to its identity. The character of the many is more than the sum total of the individual parts. Clark Williamson speaks of "individual-in-community" to describe this relationship.[10]

Human decision plays an important role in constituting the self and its relationship to community.[11] Human beings in Western cultures become most committed to participation within a community when they have an opportunity to decide who they are and what they are to do. One of the lasting legacies of modernity is critical thought: the evaluation of the strengths and weaknesses of life possibilities, and the making of a conscious selection of a possibility based on critical analysis. We become what we decide.

Marjorie Suchocki succinctly expresses the ideal relationship between individual and corporate life.

In a just society, the one and the many—the individual and the community—would relate in a mutually enriching harmony. The conditions of the society would be conducive to the well-being of the individual, making that well-being possible. As the individual freely develops in a richness of existence, that individual contributes value toward the increasing richness of society. Interdependence in relationality is a basic condition of justice. Acting for the other's good is at the same time acting for one's own good, and the impoverishment of one is the impoverishment of all.[12]

Individual and community live in dialectical relationship. Each enriching—or depriving—the other.

In postmodern perspectives, nature is a partner. Even the tiniest forms of life have their own integrity. In the optimum situation, human beings and nature live together in partnership.[13] Many in the postmodern ethos recognize that modern attitudes toward nature have created the current ecological crisis. Hence, a growing number of people feel the urgency of discovering ways by which humankind and nature can live in genuine partnership.

The church finds itself in a position to make a strong contribution as the world is moving in a postmodern direction. A desire of many in the culture (to find community) coalesces with a forceful impulse in contemporary ecclesial life (to recover the sense of the church as a community centered in unconditional love and seeking justice for all in the cosmos).

Postmodern preaching intends to form the church as community. A Christian is more than an individual with a relationship with God (and consequent personal ethical responsibilities) mediated through Jesus Christ. A Christian is an expression of a world shaped by the awareness of gracious Transcendence. And the church is more than a collection of individuals. It is a body of persons who are related to one another and to God on the analogy of the parts of the body (for instance, see 1 Cor. 12–14).

Preaching in the church in the postmodern setting needs to help the church develop as a community.

142

The Church in Relationship to Other Communities in the World

How should the church relate to the other communities in the emerging postmodern world? Christians are divided in their responses to this question.

Stanley Hauerwas and William Willimon speak for many postliberal theologians when they describe the church as a colony of resident aliens within the larger culture.[14] The church's purpose is not to attempt to transform society by engaging society on the basis of commonly recognized standards of truth and rules of discourse. Rather, the church provides a model of God's way of being community.[15] The church may join with other organizations (even secular ones) to protest war, hunger, and "other forms of inhumanity," but it does so as a part of its "proclamatory action."[16]

The sermon helps the congregation understand its role as God's colony in the world. Preaching helps the Christian community realize that its witness for God will sometimes evoke misunderstanding, and even hostility.

This view has much to commend it, especially as it preserves Christian identity and witness in a context that is often inimical to the gospel. Nonetheless, this ecclesiology has difficulties. Several of the postliberal theologians seem to regard the culture as almost inherently and unrelentingly opposed to the gospel. Some postliberals appear to give little credence to the possibility that the world may know something of God that could benefit the church. One has the sense that the ideal postliberal social world would be one in which other communities give up their own identities and join the Christian colony.[17] Some critics charge that the postliberal church is in danger of withdrawing from the larger world into its private compound. Postliberal leaders work very hard to rebut these attacks.[18] Nonetheless, even if the church does

143

not consciously withdraw from the culture, the culture can easily overlook its witness if the church does not engage the culture directly.

While I respect the postliberal version of the church, I find the revisionary church more adequate to the emerging post-modern situation and to God and the gospel. A basic task of the revisionary congregation is to learn the content of Christian tradition, and how to interpret it. Further, the revi-sionists seek for the congregation to be a public church. By public, they mean two things: (1) The church's witness (particu-larly its truth claims) can be evaluated on the basis of criteria that can be accepted by publicly acknowledged standards of truth for the day. (2) The church enters directly into the public life of the larger culture for the purpose of helping the larger culture increase its capacity to mediate love and justice for all.

In the postmodern era, the church needs to have a public charac-ter. Its standards of truth need to be pub-licly accessible. It needs to enter directly into the public life of the larger culture.

As noted in my contribution to the previous chapter, God is present throughout the culture. Christian tradition helps alert the church to points at which God is at work. Even if persons, communities, and events do not bear the name Christian, the church can still join them in their movement toward a world of love and justice. Indeed, com-munities from outside the church may come to clearer insight about God's purposes than the church. In such cases, the church can be instructed by those outside of its comradeship.

Of course, the revisionists recognize that the world is not universally revelatory of the divine presence and purpose. Many of the stories, values, and practices of the culture are distorted. Malevolent trends and events need to be critiqued.

In the broad sense, the church has a sacramental role in the world. The sacraments of baptism and the Lord's Supper are signs that assure the Christian community of God's continuous presence and love. In the same way, the church is not the only means by which God relates to the world and by which the knowledge of God comes into the world. The Christian community *represents* God's presence, and purposes.

The church has a sacramental quality in the midst of the other communities of the world. It represents the divine presence in the world in much the same way that baptism and the Lord's Supper represent the love and call of God within the church.

In the revisionary view, preaching desires to help the community effect a mutual critical correlation between Christian tradition and the contemporary church and world. The activity and character of the sermon models the whole life of the congregation. The relationship between the preacher and the congregation represents the relationship between the church and the world.

Practical Homiletical Strategies to Help Form the Church as Community

What can the preacher do to help the sermon become a community shaping event? The temptation is to say that the preacher should shift most of the pronouns in the sermon into the plural by using "we" and "us." This move is sometimes helpful. But H. H. Farmer cautions that the homiletical "we" can actually distance the congregation from the sermon. Distance develops when the use of the plural pronoun is so general that the listeners do not feel embraced by its use.[19] In order to respond positively to the homiletical "we,"

145

the congregation needs to hear their own lives and stories reflected in the sermon as a whole. And, in a community, people sometimes address one another directly, as when "I" talk directly to "you." And "I" can represent the whole community, as it sometimes did in the premodern world.

The preacher can develop an image of the sermon as a communal event. From the beginning of sermon preparation, the preacher can think of the sermon as an occasion to help the congregation develop a communal identity. This attitude may require some nurturing in the pastoral mind since most homiletics books (until recently) presupposed the sermon as addressed to the individual listener.[20] I am helped in thinking communally by asking a focal question periodically during the preparation of the sermon. "How will this sermon help the congregation as a community understand and respond to the gospel?"

To help the congregation develop as a community, the preacher can critique modern individualism, can talk about the communal aspects of Christian life, and can tell stories that illustrate the interrelatedness of the Christian community.

The act of hearing a sermon (along with sharing many other aspects of congregational life) creates a common reservoir of memory on which the community and its members can draw. Even when the specific themes of the sermon fade from conscious recall, the contents have contributed to the depths of the congregation's life. And the fact of hearing the sermon together (and of hearing many sermons over a long period of time) is itself a common bond.

Within the sermon itself, three related strategies can be especially helpful for developing communal consciousness. First, the preacher can explicitly critique the individualism that was characteristic of modernity and that permeates many minds and hearts today.[21]

146

Second, the preacher can talk about the communal dimensions of Christian identity. The pastor can help the congregation become aware of the biblical and other historic roots of Christian community. Sermons can explain the vital internal relationships by which Christians are connected. Sermons can further help the Christian community understand that (and how) it is related to other communities in the world. The pastor can provide a framework of community.

Third, the most effective way to nurture collective consciousness may be to tell stories that demonstrate the essential interrelatedness of Christians and of the Christian community to the larger world (including nature). Stories function at various levels (often simultaneously). They can illustrate a conceptual point. A narrative makes a point concrete, and shows how it relates to everyday life. A story may show how one Christian is internally related to another. Listening to a story, further, can become an experience for the congregation. The listeners identify with aspects of the setting, plot, and (or) characters, and the listeners experience the narrative as it unfolds as if they are a part of the narrative. The perspectives and events of the story thus become a part of the collective experience of the congregation. A story can create an empowering emotional fabric that is not always a part of welcoming an idea by itself. And, a story gives the congregation an image through which the congregation can perceive and act, both with respect to itself and toward other people and communities.

Today's church does not know the stories of the Bible, or the stories of Christian history. In this setting, the preacher needs to tell Bible stories and stories from history that are formative for Christian identity. Indeed, many congregations will profit from sermons whose language and structure stay very close to those of the text. Of course, the preacher also needs to help the congregation discover the significance of the stories for today's church and culture. But the congregation will be better able to determine the significance of a story (or other text) if they are first familiar with the content and intention of the text.

A reminder: it is important for the preacher to respect the complexities and ambiguities of the various communities that become focal in the sermon. The authority of the sermon is undercut when the preacher oversimplifies or paints an overly rosy picture of the nature and functioning of communities. I am weary, for instance, of sermons that romanticize nature. Nature can be beautiful. Nature and humankind are partners in cosmic community and depend upon each other for mutual survival and enrichment. But nature can also be ugly, arbitrary, untrustworthy, and savage. The authority of the sermon is increased when the preacher helps the congregation name and deal with the difficult dimensions of the natural world and its relationship with human beings. Similar complexities are true of other communities. The preacher may wax poetically about how I am joined to all others in the church. But the distasteful fact is that I do not even like all the people in the church. The trustworthiness of the sermon increases as the preacher names and helps the congregation deal with such discrepancies in its own life and in its relationship with other communities in the world.

A Perspective from Scott Black Johnston

We believe in the one holy catholic and apostolic church.
                                                        —*The Nicene Creed*

What's the Fuss?

At the hub of the most hotly contested debates in contemporary theology lie questions about ecclesiology. The issues on the table are familiar ones: What is the church? How should the church speak and act? Where does the church end and the world begin? In recent years, however, these rather basic inquiries have elicited surprisingly polemical responses. In fact, discussions related to the church have spawned calls for the return of heresy as a working term—presumably so that we might make clear what *is* and *is not* part of the Christian faith in such troubled times.[22] Why are questions about the Christian community at the center of this volatile theological moment?

Perhaps the primary reason that the church is the theological topic of the day arises out of growing perception that we are entering a "post-Christian age."[23] As the church becomes merely one among many voices in the larger culture, as Christians discover that they can no longer depend on Christendom (i.e., the supportive context of a predominantly Christian society), then the church's identity, and even survival, hinges on a community of believers that is willing to engage in constant, clear self-definition. Chiefly, then, "ecclesiology" is perched on the tips of our theological tongues, because an increasingly pluralistic world has pressed the need for Christians to articulate a compelling and faithful vision of the church. Another reason, however, that the church is at the forefront of current theological discussions can be traced to the intellectual climate fostered by postmodernity.

Provisional Foundations

In the contemporary world, the word *community* has demonstrated uncommon fortitude. Indeed, as postmodern scholarship has systematically debunked and demolished many of our other significant categories, community has managed to flourish. Why? Having dismissed the notion that there are transcendent foundations (like rationality) that can provide panoramic standards for truth, postmodern writers find that they are more and more comfortable with clearly delimited, finite—one might even say "parochial"—understandings of how the world works. Where do such parochial perceptions find their home? In community.

Community provides postmodern thinkers with a category imbued with particularity, and thus it proves to be a palatable substitute to the universality of modernity. With this idea in mind, a growing number of postmodern scholars assert that the governing principles that guide how people live and talk and act are to be found within the language, wisdom, and practice of concrete communities.[24] So, for example, rather than approach freedom as if it is a general (timeless) concept that holds sway over all humanity, postmodern thinkers prefer to talk about how specific historical communities have defined freedom. For the American revolutionaries, freedom meant relief from civil restrictions—no taxation without representation. For the slaves owned by many of these colonists, freedom meant personal liberty—broken chains and self-determination. In each case, one discerns the meaning of freedom as one studies the manner in which a particular historical community has used the word. By demonstrating the power to define both words and practices (even if it is in a provisional manner), communities have come to be viewed as rare, authoritative loci in postmodernity. For a world in which solid intellectual ground has become exceedingly scarce, communities provide viable foundations for meaningful discourse.

Church Talk

At least one strand of contemporary theology shares an appreciation for community with postmodernity.[25] Beginning with a certain (some might say "peculiar") reading of Karl Barth, a number of recent theological figures (including Hans W. Frei, George A. Lindbeck, and Stanley Hauerwas) assert that the church provides the foundation for meaningful Christian discourse.[26] Theology, for these folks, is centered around the distinctive language and practice of the Christian community. Like the postmodernists, these thinkers claim that to understand the meaning of Christian words and activities necessarily involves understanding the community in which they are at home—that is, the church.

The preacher ought not try to justify Christian claims on the basis of publicly acknowledged standards of truth. The witness of the church ought not be required to pass the muster of an authority "higher" than its own story, particularly one that may run contrary to the Christian vision.

Hence, the theological task (and, by implication, the challenge to contemporary preachers) is *not* to justify Christian words and acts in an apologetic manner, as Ron has suggested, according to the "publicly acknowledged standards of truth for the day." First of all, such standards are exceptionally difficult to locate in the postmodern world. Where are the touchstones that can be agreed upon? More theologically problematic, however, is that such appeals suggest that the witness of the church ought to pass muster with a higher authority—the courts of public rationality. Preachers committed to this judicatory run the risk that such a public forum might construe "truth" in a way that is antagonistic with the Christian principles, perhaps even going so far as to declare the primary tenets of the faith to be fraudulent. So, while Ron is correct, God can and does choose to speak through culture (remember the Athenians' undesignated altar in Acts 17:23); nevertheless, if public criteria become the final means of evaluating the truth of Christian witness, we will have delivered our faith into potentially unsympathetic hands.

Seeking to avoid such apologetic jousting, a number of cur-

The church must use its own language in order to maintain its integrity and identity. The preacher must help the Christian community learn its own language and how to use it.

rent theological projects have devoted their energies to Christian self-description. By narrating, analyzing, and clarifying how the Christian community makes use of its language and engages in its faithful practice, these projects strive to make the church the foundation of the theological enterprise.

Theological positions that assign a central role to the church have much to recommend them in this time. If by attempting to be meaningful and relevant in the cultural shuffle the language and practices of the Christian community are lost or bartered away, then the integrity and identity of the church will certainly suffer. Consider, for example, a new translation of the Bible, the *Contemporary English Version*, which proudly proclaims that it has eliminated theological words such as *justification, righteousness, redemption, reconciliation, salvation*, and even *grace* from its pages.[27] The translators have removed these terms, hoping to promote "understanding." As they explain, many of these words are not used in "everyday English." Yet this is precisely the point. Christians have (or ought to have) an exotic vocabulary. Christians engage in practices that cannot be witnessed on most street corners. So while the church should always seek to instruct those who desire to understand the language and practices of the community of faith in an *accessible* manner, that teaching must involve the appropriation of new words (ones not used in "everyday English") and participation in the distinctive practices of the faith. For preachers, this ecclesiological perspective reminds us that we have a tremendous pedagogical task before us. We are charged to teach both fledgling listeners and faithful amnesiacs how the Christian community talks and has talked throughout history.

152

Faithful Tongues

So how do Christians talk? What does it sound like when someone speaks the church's language? Some argue that the Christian vernacular sounds like verses recited from the Bible or like the stanzas of a creed (such as, "I believe in God the Father Almighty"). Others equate the language of the church with the doctrinal positions and liturgical practices common to their denomination (for instance, "we Presbyterians understand the eucharist to be . . ."). Still others suggest that a true manifestation of the Christian language can be found only in particular parishes (for example, each year on the second Sunday of Advent Mrs. Simmons stands and reads her poem about John the Baptist). So while it is easy to talk in an abstract manner about the Christian church as the foundation of our faithful talk (and even our preaching), it quickly becomes apparent—when faced with the reality of a living, breathing historical church—that there is no *one* language spoken by all faithful Christians. This realization delivers a critical nudge to those who think that all we need to do is say "church" and we have wiggled our way out of any theological confusion, for the church is an incredibly complicated entity.

The fact that the church exists on so many levels and can be found in so many diverse forms raises pivotal questions for the contemporary preacher. Is each Christian community an authority in and of itself and therefore justified in whatever it says and does? Or is the "official" church (i.e., the denominational offices, the creedal statements, or perhaps the diocesan bishops) the true purveyor of faithful Christian language? Both of these options prove troublesome. The first leads to a community-based relativism. Mere existence as a community is not a ticket to God's favor. We must not forget that the scriptures are replete with stories about particular communities that incurred God's wrath because of their unjust practices and evil ways. Clearly, for Christians, authority is not (as postmodern thinkers suggest) simply the internal creation of a historical community; it is a trust from Christ. Individual churches have authority in this world only to the extent that they bear witness to the Resurrected One. The same criterion holds for higher levels of ecclesial authority. Moreover, the danger in locating "true" Christian language solely in overarching ecclesial powers and documents is that these authorities are not always familiar with the particularity of individual congregations. Accordingly, they are not necessarily attuned to the specific preaching context that plays such a crucial role in determining what it means to speak and act in a faithful manner. In other words, faithful Christian language in East Los Angeles will not sound exactly like faithful Christian language in Eau Claire, Wisconsin. This recognition provides a clue for pastors who hope to ground their faithful preaching within the multifaceted Body of Christ.

The Legacy of Pentecost

At first glance, both the catholicity and unity confessed within the Nicene Creed seem far from the church's grasp in the postmodern world. So what's a preacher to do? First we need to be reminded that the miracle of Pentecost was not that everyone suddenly spoke the same language, but that people of different nationalities heard and understood the gospel in their own native tongue. This narrative suggests that faithful preaching

Each congregation tells the Christian story in ways that are specific to that community. The preacher needs to learn and speak the language of that community. The preacher needs also to gauge the degree to which a

requires that a pastor first engage in faithful hearing. To preach a word that is relevant to a community's life in Christ requires that a pastor listen to the language of scripture and tradition with ears shaped by these particular people. Martin Luther records the story of one of his students who spent considerable time in a sermon railing against the evils of wet-nursing (i.e., hiring oneself out to suckle another woman's child). Luther intimates that the student might have preached a more fitting word if he had paid more attention to his preaching context—a congregation in which no person in attendance was under the age of sixty.

particular community's telling of the story is adequate to the larger Christian narrative.

The church is formed by our common experience of grace and is held together by gratitude for that grace. The experience directly contrasts with the culture of democracy, which is held together by the desire to protect and maximize individual rights.

The contemporary preacher is called to walk a fine line, balancing the integrity of Christianity's unique words and acts with the challenge to speak a word that is addressed to a specific historical people. How is this delicate task to be accomplished? This inquiry pushes us on to the next chapter devoted to homiletical theory, yet in so doing we will not leave the church behind. If anthropology was the key to the last homiletical movement (i.e., How do individual human beings listen?), ecclesiology is the key to the next phase in preaching theory (i.e., How is my preaching faithful both to the gospel of Jesus Christ and to the specific Christian community that I have been called to serve?).

A Perspective from Barbara Blaisdell

The church is called together by Jesus Christ with a mission to tell the world about God's unbounded love. The church is a community whose identity is primarily formed by our experience of grace and held together by our gratitude for that grace. This is in direct contrast to that which holds the culture of democracy together: the protection and maximization of individual rights. It is our gratitude for grace that shapes how the church community responds to individuals within it and to the world beyond it. It is therefore the case that the church community has an identity and a language that differs from the world at large. But given our calling as a missionary community, we cannot avoid offering a public defense of such language. Because we are called to live in the

An excerpt from a sermon uses the story of the encounter of the ten lepers with Jesus to reflect on the relationship between individual and community in the Christian community.

world and speak to the world, we cannot and ought not avoid conversation with the public values of the world. By conversation, I mean a mutual critical correlation of Christian and public values. Anything less is triumphalism and not conversation. Consider the story of the encounter of the ten lepers and Jesus as recorded in Luke 17:11-19.

Most of the stories in the Gospels about people who encounter Jesus are about an individual person. But this story stands by itself in being not about a single individual, but about a group of people who are standing in the same place because they are standing in a common need. This little congregation of ten may be composed of very different individuals, but they can stand together now because they know they all need something. And they look at Jesus from a distance and wave and say, "Lord, have mercy. Help us." Such is not a particularly popular recognition in our culture: the fact that I am a person in need of mercy. The culture of democratic individualism prefers to emphasize my ability and not my need, my rights and not my gratitude for wrongs righted.

The particular need of the people of this story was to be healed of leprosy, one of the most awful and feared diseases of Jesus' day. Many people today have made a connection between leprosy and HIV/AIDS. But the particular need isn't really what matters. What matters is how many of us have such a need, how many of us belong in the company of those who are calling for help. One of the things the church owes the world is the recognition that *we are as needy as the world*. We are neither above nor beyond world citizenship.

Among the group of ten about which Luke tells, are some folks who used to mistrust one another, who would not have lowered themselves to talk to one another. In that circle were old racial enemies: Samaritans and Jews. But it's funny how all those old divisions don't matter anymore. They don't matter when you know that where you really belong is in the fellowship of need and suffering. We dare not mind too much who stands beside us when we ask for help, whether it be secular humanists, fundamentalists, liberals, postliberals and revisionists, or even folks who hold positions contrary to the gospel. We all are standing in a circle of need.

> **Community begins when human beings recognize that we all stand in a common circle of need.**

Jesus gives an answer to these people who cry for help. But to people like us, his answer is really a shock, because he doesn't say anything like, "Children, I know how much it hurts" or "Tell me more about your pain." He doesn't say a tender word. He doesn't even come a step closer to them. He doesn't touch them or tell them, "Now, I've healed you." All he says is "Go!" And it sounds like a stern command. *Go!* Jesus never did take that course in pastoral care—or else he flunked it. Sometimes you need comfort, but what you get is a commandment. This story suggests that sometimes the need for healing is not best answered with soft words, but with the hearing and obeying of a new commandment.

"Go and show yourselves to the priests," he said. Now that's what a leper did *after* he had been healed. You went to the priest who checked you over and told you you were all right. The ten lepers are not cured. But Jesus commands them to act *as if* they were cured. He won't hand them a healing, but he will give them something to do on faith. In other words, he'll honor them with a partnership in their own healing. And that is the meaning of all of God's commandments. What we call the "law" is really God's gracious insistence that we take the steps that are our part in getting well.

The ten decide to trust the grace of a commandment. Though not cured, they act as if they might be by being obedient. We dare not forget the order of these steps toward healing the church. We act as if we might be cured by being obedient to the gospel. We dare not presume we already are cured even with the gospel in our hands. As the story goes, when the lepers go and do what they had been commanded, they discover they are all wearing new skin.

One reason I like this story so much is because it is much more like the experience I have with healing. Some of the Gospel stories seem to imply that a healing from God comes instantly. But most of us don't get better all of a sudden. Real transformations almost always occur somewhere down the road, somewhere between a word we heard and our destination. We'd like to be fixed right now. Our culture would tell us we have a right to be fixed right now. But the reality of our experience is that the fixing almost always happens down the road of being faithful.

It happens this way for the ten lepers. Somewhere along the way of going where they were commanded, they discover that their flesh has been restored, fresh as a child's—

perfect, unblemished skin. And they do what I think just about any of us would do when headed down the highway with a brand new life. They accelerate.
Jesus had told them to go. Going made them better. What are new feet for, if not to sprint to the finish of what we've been told to do? "Go to the priests then, and step on it!"

The outsider—the Samaritan—helps us recognize qualities that make for genuine, inclusive community.

But one of the ten breaks stride, slows down, stops, then turns completely around. He is suddenly in no hurry to see his priest. He's got something wilder than compliance on his mind. He's got new skin. He's got a new life. This needs and wants a new voice. He has to *do* something here! So he runs the other way, praising God with a loud voice, and then he falls at the feet of Jesus and says, "Thank you. Thank you!"

Here Luke adds a piece of information we haven't had until now. The tenth leper was a Samaritan. He has been cleansed from the stigma of leprosy, but he's still wearing the stigma of race. All through his life he's going to be an outcast, even though he's been cured of leprosy. But it is he, the outcast, who has come back to pour out his praise. Jesus says, "Mmm, weren't there ten? Where are the nine?" Well there's a perfectly obvious answer to that question. The nine are out doing exactly what Jesus told them to do. They are doing their duty.

Maybe part of what keeps these nine guys running and doing their duty is their eagerness to be certified. That's what the priests are going to give them, you know. And with their certification of cure, all their memberships will be reinstated, all their rights restored. Maybe a Samaritan, an outcast, knows not to trust that stuff so much. Maybe he knows that the establishment can't give him anything that matters. If a public theology is primarily motivated by the need for certification, it will fail. If a public theology is motivated by the need to communicate God's love, it will be faithful.

In our culture, gratitude is one of the most significant things a public theology must communicate. Common gratitude for God's goodness and grace is a key to forming community that is whole.

One of the most significant things a public theology must communicate, especially in this culture, is gratitude. We need to remind ourselves and to give witness in the world to our gratitude for the abundance of God's grace in our lives. And here's the thing: until we find ourselves there, we don't find ourselves whole. As a church, as individuals, we can run down the road of doing all the right things for the world—and, of course, we ought to do them! Feed the hungry. Clothe the naked. Visit the imprisoned. We owe the world these things. But while doing these as commanded will make us better, they will not make us whole until we come to the place of wild, gratuitous praise for the grace we have received. Jesus gave ten healings that day. Everybody got new skin. But it was the one who poured out praise at Jesus' feet who heard Jesus say, "Your faith has made you whole."

Sometimes I think we, as the church, look to all the world like nine dutiful lepers trying to do the right thing—half-whole people trying to do the right stuff to get someone's approval Where's the *one* who wheels around for the wildness of love's beauty in return? That gratitude for the gospel is what sets us apart as we converse with the world.

Modes of Discourse for the Sermon in the Postmodern World

A Perspective from Ronald Allen

T he preacher steps to the pulpit, straightens her notes, clears her throat, looks into the faces of the congregation, and begins the sermon. What happens when the preacher speaks and the congregation listens? And how do various homiletical forms (or structures, or rhetorical styles) affect the communication that takes place in a sermon? Preaching textbooks increasingly point to close ties between *what* the preacher says and *how* the preacher says it. Are some modes of discourse better suited than others to a congregation in an increasingly postmodern setting?

Earlier Views of Language

We must be careful not to oversimplify, or romanticize, premodern views of language. Scholars, particularly in the field of preaching, are fond of claiming that premodern communities believed that language had power and that words were agents that could bring to pass that which they spoke. These qualities could be true under certain conditions. For instance, Isaiah's God says, "For as the rain and the snow come down from heaven, and do not return there until they have watered the earth, making it bring forth and sprout, giving seed to the sower and bread to the eater, so shall my word be that goes out from my mouth; it shall not return to me empty, but it shall accomplish that which I purpose, and succeed in the thing for which I sent it" (Isa. 55:10-11).

However, while this use of language is the norm for deity, it is not always so for human beings. Anthony C. Thistleton has discovered that language functioned in multiple ways in premodern communities.[1] Among human beings, language seldom had irreversible or magical qualities. No single theory of language can account for premodern speech. Nonetheless, even if premodern uses of language did not have universally the romantic qualities attached to them by professors of preaching, it appears to me that premodern people had a greater sense of the liveliness and importance of speaking than do many people today. And aspects of premodern speech are important to our discussion.

Many premodern communities spoke extensively in mythic stories. A purpose of most premodern myths is to help the community understand why things are the way they are. Myths answer questions such as, How did the world get here? What is the purpose of life? Why are things the way they are? Why do things happen in the world as they do? Myth imparts assurance as it locates the community in relationship to ultimate (and penultimate) realities.

The preacher in the premodern world spoke the language of the tradition. A major work of the sermon was to initiate the congregation into the language of the tradition and to explain its significance. The preacher helped the community learn its stories and the vocabulary by which it understood God and the world. The preacher sought to show how the language of the tradition applied to new situations. Preachers often made use of commonly known and accepted rhetorical styles, such as oracles of judgment, oracles of salvation, the diatribe.

Modern linguists differentiated between propositional (factual) and mythic (fanciful) uses of language. The former was accurate and trustworthy. The latter was primitive and not reliable.

The modern world distinguished between two uses of language: propositional and mythic. Propositional language corresponded to reality in a one-to-one way. Having science and philosophy as its models, it provided information about the realities of which it spoke.

Mythic language was regarded by many moderns as primitive. Myth was based in nonscientific, nonrational perceptions of reality. At its best, mythic speech clothed truth in fanciful (and frequently misleading) garments.

To be sure, the modern world preserved a place for the aesthetic uses of metaphorical speech, as in poetry. And moderns valued imaginative stories (e.g., the modern world generated many novels). But the thoroughly modern reader tended to regard imaginative language in the form of poetry or novel as the container of propositional meaning. Hence, in English class, we would read a poem, dissect its figures of speech, and then state its meaning in propositional language.

The modern church conceived of the sermon as the exposition of a proposition. The preacher needed to present and explain an idea to the congregation. A major purpose of the sermon was to provide accurate information about God, the world, and Christian life, and to persuade the congregation of the truth of the sermon's claims. Along the way, the preacher might tell stories to illustrate the proposition or to add interest to the sermon, but the stories were subsidiary to the propositon.

If the sermon dealt with a biblical text or a Christian doctrine that was narrative in form or that contained mythic (or other nonscientific) elements, the preacher would isolate the propositional summary of the meaning of the passage. The proposition of the text could become the basis of the sermon.

Multiple Modes of Discourse in the Postmodern Situation

Stenic and tensive uses of language each have their own strengths and weaknesses. The preacher must be able to speak in both modes.

The preacher in the postmodern church is coming to a homiletical promised land in these matters. The preacher inherits significant dimensions of both premodern and modern understandings of language but transcends them both.[2] Taking a cue from modernity, many today regard language as functioning in two ways. These two functions go by various names.[3] For purposes of discussion, I borrow Philip Wheelwright's terms: *stenic* and *tensive*.

Stenic language is propositional and informational.[4] It is salutary for certain tasks. It assumes correspondence between language and reality. It communicates data with precision.

The great value of stenic language is that it can be very precise.

Typically, stenic language appeals to the intellect. This type of language is very useful. It helps people communicate about basic life matters with ease and accuracy.

Stenic language allows philosophers, theologians, and preachers to state plainly what they believe (and what Christians can and cannot believe). When the congregation is struggling to identify a Christian perspective on a contemporary social issue, stenic speech can frequently help the congregation enumerate the various options for interpreting the issue and the reasons for each.

But the stenic use of language can also be limiting. Some matters suffer severe loss of meaning when they are boiled down to simple factual statement. Some language is polyvalent (or multivalent). Such language has more than one meaning than can be identified at any given time. A stenic summary of such language (particularly various kinds of texts) practically never represents the fullness of the texts.

Tensive language, as its name implies, embodies the tensions that are a part of life process. When we receive (and use) tensive speech, we experience (at least to a degree) tensions apropos the content of the language, such as between the self and God, between the self and other persons, between "one's impulses and rational thought," between a community's actual situation and its possible situations, between the community and the environment. As we grope to express the complex nature of the world, we create language that "give[s] some hint, always finally insufficient, of the turbulent moods within and the turbulent world of qualities and forces, promises and threats, outside."[5] People who use and receive such language are touched at all levels of their beings—intellect, feeling, will.

> **Tensive language can reflect, and create, the tensions with which life is charged.**

Tensive language is often found in types of expression that we associate with the arts—novels, poems, short stories, words set to music. But we can encounter tensive speech in almost any mode of discourse, for almost any mode of discourse can manifest tensive qualities. Tensiveness is less a function of genre and more a result of the use to which language is put.

The tensive view regards language as an active agent. It has the power to accomplish that which it speaks. Hearing (and using) tensive expression touches us at the deepest levels so that the tensions embodied in the language are released in us. In this vein, a movement has taken energy in the last forty years around the extraordinary power of language. Language performs that which it speaks. Words are deeds in the sense that words can effect that which they speak.[6]

At its most potent, language has the power to effect that which it speaks. In the broad sense, language creates world.

To recall another famous expression, postmoderns sometimes say that language creates world.[7] By this expression, they mean that the language that we use shapes our perception of the world. It orients us to meaning and value. It names the good and the bad. It prescribes behavior. Language clues the congregation to the nature of its relationships with others in the world, and it helps the community have a measure of control in its relationships. In short, language furnishes the interpretive grid by which we come to understand the world. In this regard, the postmodern view of language recollects one of the most important functions of premodern speech: it names the world.

Postmodern linguists make three valuable observations about myth: (1) They often regard myth as tensive. A narrative myth uses setting, characters, plot, and personification to represent a community's feeling about the world and its place in it. (2) People of nearly every culture live on the basis of myth; that is, nearly every culture is founded upon its own set of stories (and assumptions) that locate it in the midst of time and space. Modernity's view of science as the exalted source of knowledge has mythic qualities. (3) The mythic underpinnings of a community may be explicit or implicit. In the explicit case, the community consciously lives on the basis of stories, ideas, values, and practices that are known, told, and practiced. For instance, the church seeks to remember (or learn) the formative stories of the Bible and the Christian tradition. In the implicit case, the community may not consciously remember its stories, ideas, or values in a fully developed form. Nonetheless, the mythic substrata are communicated through the ethos of the community, through figures of speech, through everyday behavior, through tone of voice. The implicit mythology is often more powerful than the explicit one.

Tensive language typically is best received in its own medium. Susanne K. Langer points out that tensive (presentational) language is intended to be presented directly to the gestalt.[8] We hear a story as a story, and a poem as a poem. We watch a play. We feel the force of a proverb as a proverb. The language creates patterns of feelings and associations that are an integral part of the depth dimensions of the meaning of the language event.

To be sure, a listener sometimes needs explanatory comments to clarify aspects of what is being said. Such comments are especially useful in the case of literature from other times and places whose language and cultural assumptions are not familiar. Exegesis can open up the world of a text.

Language cannot always be neatly classified into stenic or tensive categories. Tensive language can grow stale, sedimented, and stenic with overuse or trivialization. For example, in its better moments, the parable of the good Samaritan (Luke 10:25-37) causes its listeners to call into question the restrictions

Postmodern people recognize that language functions in many different ways. The same event of speaking and hearing can even function differently for different people. The preacher needs to be alert to the various ways in which language might be received and to shape the message accordingly.

that they place on divine love. But through repetition and reductionism, that parable is today (to many) only an example of nice behavior. "You should be a good Samaritan."

Speech that would ordinarily be used and received stenically can function tensively when it sparks awareness of the depth processes of life. For instance, my interior life is frequently electrified when I come upon a fresh theological proposition (or a fresh statement of an old statement). One of the preacher's responsibilities is to try to create sermonic

When the sermon has tensive qualities, it becomes an event. The hearing of the sermon adds to the congregation's reservoir of experience. conditions under which language can function in its optimum mode.

Much of the Bible, and many elements of Christian doctrine and tradition, are tensive. Biblical texts, and Christian doctrine and tradition, provide more than information about God. Such material can evoke, disclose, or create the awareness of the realities of which they speak.

Tensive language can add to our world. For by participating in the language event, something really happens to us. Susanne Langer's observation about stories is true of tensive speech generally. "The 'livingness' of a story is really much surer, and often greater" than things that happen to us day to day. "Life itself may, at times, be quite mechanical and unperceived by those who live it, but the perception of a reader must never fall into abeyance."[9] Freed from the distractions that often are a part of everyday existence, we can focus on the language event itself. In so doing, we can experience the world from the standpoint of the text, doctrine, or other Christian speech. Language can cause us to feel things that we have never felt before.

Paul Ricoeur describes a three-phase hermeneutical engagement between preacher and text (and other elements of tradition) that captures the transition from the modern to the postmodern epochs in language.[10] In phase one, the preacher encounters the text naively. The preacher assumes the validity of the text. In phase two, the preacher puts the text into the fire of critical reflection, discerning the distance in culture and worldview between the text and the contemporary community. The preacher particularly notes points at which the text makes a positive contribution to the life of the community, and points at which the text is problematic for the community. In phase three, the preacher is able to return to many texts in a second naiveté.[11] In this phase, the preacher and the congregation use the language of text to name the world but recognize its limitations.

In the deep sense of truth and knowledge (as discussed in chapters 3 and 4), myth, and other imaginative expressions of the Christian faith, can be true. The details of biblical stories may not be factually objective from the modern standpoint. But the experience represented in the text is true to our experience.[12] Some details of the story of the Exodus may not be factually verifiable, but in this deep sense the story corresponds with our experience of transcendent reality as ultimately benevolent and liberating. The story helps us name the contemporary presence, purposes, and power of God.

The preacher, then, understands the sermon not as a bulletin board that posts information about God, world, and church, but as an event. Things really happen during the sermon. Indeed, the sermon can become a world where the congregation enters the perceptual sphere of the sermon and discovers life from the perspective of the gospel.

The Homiletical Smorgasbord in the Postmodern Ethos

The preacher can use both stenic and tensive language. The Bible, the tradition, and the contemporary world offer the preacher a large variety of forms for the sermon. Critical consciousness is one of the irreversible gains of modernity. Hence, the preacher is always on the bubble to consider which kinds of discourse seem most appropriate for a given sermon (or a given part of a sermon).[13]

Sermons typically have their best effects when they speak to and for a particular community. This means that one of the preacher's tasks is to identify the listening profile of the congregation. What types of language are most communicative in the

Given the diversity of the characteristics of listeners in the postmodern ethos, no single homiletical formula can guide the preparation of every sermon. The preacher must decide both what to say and how best to say it in the light of the subject matter, the intended effect of the sermon, and the particular qualities of listener participation in the congregation.

congregation? In keeping with the postmodern themes of plurality and diversity, recent studies of listeners and learners show that people receive and process information in different ways.[14] Some people are most comfortable with propositional preaching and have difficulty processing tensive language. They need for the preacher to spell out the sermon's point and its applicability to life. Other listeners are impatient with stenic speech and are engaged by more imaginative modes of discourse. A lot of people seem to respond to a combination of stenic and tensive language.

Questions such as the following may prove helpful as a part of the preacher's exegesis of the congregation. What kinds of discourse does the community receive most easily? Which do they find most difficult? Which do they resist? To be sure, every congregation contains people all along the listening spectrum. But congregations often develop personalities and patterns (much as individuals do).[15] In such cases, a significant percentage of the congregation may develop a preference for a certain type of speech. The preacher can make use of this way of speaking, while being careful to preach in a variety of styles that embrace the whole community.

Preachers, too, develop preferred patterns of preaching. My observation from teaching preaching for thirteen years is that most preachers prefer inductive, imaginative homiletical styles. But, in response to critical reflection on the listening climate in the congregation, preachers may need to make a conscientious effort to preach in modes beyond their preferences.

170

When the preacher communicates in a mode that is congenial to the thought processes of the congregation, the listeners are more receptive than when the sermon is conveyed in a way that is foreign to (or that annoys) those in the locus of preference.

Different modes of discourse can serve different needs in the congregation. By "needs," I have in mind a double reference. At one level, needs include those things for which the congregation itself has conscious desire. At another level, the needs include those things which the congregation requires if it is to function optimally as a Christian community. The congregation may or may not feel these latter needs, but the preacher must address them if the congregation is to have a healthy Christian life and witness.

Many congregations today are not well acquainted with the Bible or the history of the church or with basic Christian doctrines. Hence, one of the most important functions of the sermon is to help the congregation learn (or recall) the formative stories, texts, doctrines, and concepts of the Christian tradition. Some preaching in churches moving into the postmodern world should have an informational dimension. However, given the polyvalent character of language, sermons that appear to be stenic can well become tensive as "information" about the Christian life makes contact with the life processes of the congregation.

As one would expect in an era that emphasizes plurality, the current homiletical scene is a smorgasbord of approaches to the sermon. I mention several of the most popular.

- Fred Craddock's inductive preaching has become a symbol of the creativity and freedom of the new era in preaching styles.[16]
- Edmund Steimle, Morris Niedenthal, and Charles Rice envision the sermon as story.[17]

171

- Eugene Lowry sees the sermon as a five-phase homilet-ical plot (upsetting the equilibrium, analyzing the discrepancy, disclosing the clue to resolution, experiencing the gospel, anticipating the consequences). [18]
- Henry Mitchell thinks of the sermon as an experience of the gospel that culminates in celebration.[19]
- David Buttrick posits the sermon as a plot made up of a series of carefully connected moves.[20]
- Thomas G. Long and Sidney Greidanus take the lead in letting the literary form of a biblical passage shape the form of the sermon. The sermon moves in the perception of the hearers (both the explicit and implicit realms of perception) in the same way that the text moves.[21]
- Paul Scott Wilson highlights the importance of imagination in preaching (while holding an important place for conceptual thought).[22]
- Thomas Troeger sees the sermon as the movement of a series of images.[23]
- The oral-aural nature of the sermon is receiving a hearing.[24]
- A recent proposal speaks of the sermon as conversation.[25]
- A theologically credible topical sermon is even making a comeback.[26]

In addition, the preacher can create a form for a sermon for a particular occasion. The possibilities for structuring a sermon are limited only by the preacher's imagination.

The preacher's task is to analyze the relationship of the gospel, the occasion, the needs of the congregation, and the patterns of speaking and listening preferred by the community. Through critical reflection, the preacher seeks to answer the question: What mode(s) of discourse seems most likely to best serve the situation in which the sermon will come to life?

A Perspective from Scott Black Johnston

English-speaking tourists abroad are inclined to believe that if only they speak English loudly and distinctly and slowly enough, the natives will know what's being said even though they don't understand a single word of the language. Preachers often make the same mistake. They believe that if only they will speak the ancient verities loudly and distinctly and slowly enough, their congregations will understand them. Unfortunately, the only language people really understand is their own language, and unless preachers are prepared to translate the ancient verities into it, they might as well save their breath.[27]

—Frederick Buechner

The questions of the truthfulness of Christian convictions cannot be abstracted from the ecclesial and moral context.[28]

—Stanley Hauerwas

Does It Fit?

In the first chapter of this book, the movie *Pulp Fiction* served to illustrate the notion that the postmodern world is a context within which contemporary preachers endeavor to speak a faithful word. So, perhaps it is appropriate as we contemplate *how* pastors should preach given the climate of postmodernity, that we conclude by considering another product of American cinema—*Apollo 13*. The plot of Ron Howard's movie revolves around the true story of three astronauts who face the prospect that they will be marooned in outer space. The narrative ticks down the hours as the men struggle to effect some difficult—perhaps impossible—repairs on their spacecraft.

At one particularly tense juncture, the astronauts discover that they are quickly running out of breathable air. The round filter that scrubs their oxygen has reached its capacity, and the only replacement is square in shape. Responding to this crisis at mission control, the director of operations grabs a box of *everything* that the astronauts have available to them in their capsule (things like duct tape, socks, and plastic notebook covers) and runs to a room where several engineers wait. "Folks," he says, holding up a version of the square filter and the round receptacle, "you have one hour to make this fit into this using only these materials."

Each week in preparing to preach, the pastor is faced with a similar dilemma. Like the engineers whose objective was to restore breathable air to the capsule, preachers have one life-sustaining goal in mind—to proclaim the gospel. Yet, we often find that things do not fit together as neatly as we had hoped. As the week moves along, no clear, analogous connection between the lectionary-assigned biblical text and the congregation's life may come to mind.[29] Perhaps the method of sermon composition that was supposed to be keyed to universal patterns of human listening seems unable to capture the attention of an all-too-concrete congregation. Maybe, this same homiletical strategy betrays the rhetorical shape of the scriptural passage under scrutiny (for instance, the biblical text wants to confront, while the sermon form seems to cajole). What do preachers do when they are caught week after week by such dilemmas? Like the engineers in *Apollo 13*, we improvise. We use our faithful imaginations to piece together sermons that take account of the many changing variables that confront us.[30]

Ron reflects the drift of recent homiletical theory when he suggests that preachers should choose a mode of discourse that best serves a particular situation. I think that he (and others who agree) are heading in a right direction; so,

I want to affirm, but expand, his position. A preacher is called to craft a word particular to a specific congregation. Consequently, she or he must be willing to study, adapt, and sometimes discard standard homiletical forms and structures that (in the name of the

Homiletics has long been asking "How do people listen?" That question should be preceded by a more important one: "Who listens?"

universal listener) do not take account of the concrete gathering of worshipers to whom one speaks. To make such strategic theological decisions, however, requires that preachers change their focus. In pursuing the question, "How do humans listen?" we have neglected a prior, theologically important question, "Who listens?"

The question "Who listens?" is an important one as we enter the next phase of homiletics. First, it grounds preaching in a theological context. Who listens? The church listens. And the church has a theological vocabulary to describe those who listen: the baptized, the catechumens, the sinful, the saved, and the unbelieving. These terms and others describe theological identity, the missing critical component in contemporary preaching theory. Second, the question "Who listens?" also compels us to pursue anthropological examinations in a more faithful manner. By embedding our task first in an ecclesial framework, this question invites preachers to evaluate the anthropological facets of the task of preaching through theological lenses. Hence, instead of speculating about the universal characteristics of listeners (macro-anthropology), preachers are called upon to do specific cultural, psychological, economic, and social analysis in the context of a worshiping community (micro-anthropology in a theological perspective). Who listens? Particular people with particular histories in particular churches. To preach faithfully requires that we take these particularities into account.

A Promising Trajectory

Aspects of contemporary homiletics have already begun to take strides in this direction. For example, Thomas G. Long argues that "every sermon form, then, must be custom tailored to match the particular preaching occasion."[31] "Sermons," writes Fred Craddock, "are not speeches for all occasions but are rather addresses prepared for one group at a particular time and place."[32] Christine M. Smith also articulates a version of this theme. She describes the preacher as a theologian—immersed in the particularities of the world and the mysteries of the faith—who is called to discern and then to proclaim. "The very act of preaching situates the preacher in the midst of the mysterious and perplexing nature of life and faith, trying to discern and proclaim the nature of God, the nature of human existence, the nature of the relationship between God and humanity, and the nature of human responsibility for creation."[33] These three preachers each recognize the extent to which faithful sermons arise out of the flow of a particular congregation's life. Accordingly, each week's sermon preparation, to borrow homiletician John McClure's helpful imagery, must embody a unique "conversation" between the biblical text and the lives of the listeners—a conversation that cannot be adequately anticipated Sunday after Sunday by any one sermon design strategy.[34]

So, as preachers work to prepare each sermon—to use the language of the Christian tradition, the scriptures, and the world in an intelligible manner—they need to look to the particularities of their worshiping communities. Determining how to preach faithfully takes the flow of life in a congregation—including the changing, rule-based patterns that provide for the meaningful use of language—into account. This is *not* to say that preaching necessarily conforms itself to localized patterns of language use; instead, it is to argue that preachers must regard them as important. Relativism is not the answer; relevance is! That is to say, preachers must be concerned with both the faithful language of the church and the way in which particular Christian communities talk. For ultimately, the truth of the gospel must be both carefully discerned and boldly proclaimed in concrete contexts.

The preacher's vocation includes discerning the particular ways in which a congregation understands and speaks the gospel.

The constant task of the preacher is to discern the gospel given the variances of congregation, biblical text, tradition, and world. No one sermon design strategy or mode of discourse can take account of these shifting aspects in the way that the preacher on the spot is called to do. Nevertheless, different homiletical strategies (along with different exegetical methods and other resources from the Christian tradition) will continue to be the tools of the preacher's trade. By using the appropriate homiletical tools (that is, ones that fit the biblical text and the situation at hand) the preacher, a practical theologian at work, is able to craft a faithful sermon in which the particularity of God's word to a given gathering of listeners in a distinctive moment of history echoes.

Whose Words?

All of this is to argue that, when held in tension, the statements made by Stanley Hauerwas and Frederick Buechner (quoted at the beginning of this chapter) can provide us with an accurate picture of the preacher's task.

The language of the sermon should echo the language of the church, the language of God's self-revelation in Jesus Christ.

Hauerwas reminds us that the truthfulness of Christian preaching can be abstracted neither from the church nor from the unique language associated with God's self-revelation in Jesus Christ. As the Body of Christ, the church provides the context in which preaching makes sense—even missionary preaching. For when faithful preaching is done—even outside the four walls of an ecclesial structure—it is done within the context of Christ's church. It arises out of scripture, is shaped by our confessions, and is surrounded,

The gospel of Jesus Christ is never generic. It is always a particular message to particular people. As such, preaching is paradigmatic of how Christians talk.

supported, and filled, in every aspect and at every juncture, by the spirit of our God, the spirit of Pentecost that continues to create communities of believers, the spirit that even in the face of Christianity's mind-boggling diversity calls us to confess "one holy, catholic, and apostolic church."

Yet, to paraphrase Buechner, we simply cannot hope that speaking the important doctrines of the church with greater and greater volume will eventually result in understanding. Preachers need to take account of the way in which people in their particular church use language; we need to pay attention to the rules that shape the language of the communities in which we find ourselves. For the gospel of Jesus Christ is never a generic gospel; it is always a particular word spoken to a particular group of people. As such, preaching is a paradigmatic illustration of how Christians talk. We struggle to express the God of the Pentateuch in words that make sense in downtown Dallas, rural Maine, or the suburbs of Mexico City. We proclaim the good news of Jesus Christ while making use of language that is also spoken in the office, the laundromat, and the pool hall. We speak words like "grace," "sin," and "gospel," knowing full well that somehow our culture has gotten hold of these signs, changed the rules, and corrupted their theological use. We are faced with the fact that the boundaries between church-talk and "secular" language are quite blurred. As Long puts it, we enter "into the middle of the conversation, and people are out there in the pews (and in the world) already wondering about God and talking about God."[35] In this situation, we are called to preach; and to preach intelligibly in this milieu is to take theological account of the community-embedded rules that describe how words are to be used meaningfully.

Who speaks in the sermon? God takes the words and makes them into The Word.

The danger that some suspect is lurking behind the exhortation that the preachers should pay attention to the way in which a particular church and a particular community—is that such a claim gives slight to the vertical claim of preaching (i.e., the God who speaks continually afresh through the words of the sermon). This is not the case. As Craddock writes:

> The preacher takes the words provided by the culture and tradition, selects from among them those that have the qualities of clarity, vitality, appropriateness, arranges them so as to convey the truth and evoke interest, pronounces them according to the best accepted usage, and offers them to God in the sermon. It is God who fashions words into the Word.[36]

Logos

In every corner of the world, in every context (be it modernity, postmodernity, or whatever follows), we who preach are called to tell the story of Christ—clearly, compellingly, ceaselessly. To do so requires a conviction about the church's distinctive language, but it also compels us to pay attention to the way in which individual Christian communities talk. For it is in blending our vernacular words with the language of salvation that we are true to our God—the one who in preaching along the shores of Galilee described the "kingdom of heaven" as a "bulging net" and who called the disciples to fish for people.

Preaching is analogous to the Incarnation: it is Word become flesh in a particular situation.

Finally, as we craft our sermons with love and care, we must remember that God is not merely the object of our preaching, a dose of theological content poured into homiletical form, but the Subject who proclaims. As we speak words of scripture, recall promises passed down through Christian traditions, and utter sentences tailored to particular communities, God the active subject in Christian proclamation again encounters us as the Word. Again and again, preaching shows itself to be analogous to the person of Jesus Christ. For preaching is invariably incarnational; it is the Logos that has put on the particularities of (and indeed become one with) human speech. Preaching is nothing less than God risking an encounter with humankind, week after week, in pulpits and on street corners. The Word continually becomes flesh for us.

A Perspective from Barbara Blaisdell

John Updike, in his latest novel, *In the Beauty of the Lilies*, tells the story of Clarence Wilmot, a Presbyterian clergyman of the early twentieth century who, while reading Ingersoll's *Some Mistakes of Moses* in order to refute its atheism for a troubled parishioner, finds his own faith escape upward and away from him. He becomes convinced that Ingersoll is right, that "the God of the Pentateuch was an absurd bully, barbarically thundering through the cosmos entirely misconceived. There is no such God, nor should there be."[37]

When he seeks to resign his ministry in response to his conscience, Wilmot is accused by his wife of selfishness. In a troubling interview with the moderator of his presbytery, Wilmot is admonished to remain in ministry despite his doubts. The moderator argues that "unfaith is a cohort of faith."[38] The moderator is articulate (or glib, depending on one's interpretation) regarding modern theological issues of truth and faith. He offers a constructive and forthright response to the pastor's questions. But the conversation is nevertheless troubling and his arguments are rendered far less effective than they might be because he fails to acknowledge the real ethical pull on Reverend Wilmot: to be true to himself and his unbelief, to be honest about what is and is not going on inside him.

The novel traces four succeeding generations of the Wilmot family and their connection to and longing for faith. In the end, both faith and absence of faith fail to heal or save. Both fail to address the powerful ethical claims of the other, and that failure is at the root of the Branch Davidian-like end of the novel. Updike calls us to reflect upon this profound division in our culture between the competing claims of the secular and the sacred and our failure to learn from each other. I longed for a character who could bridge the gap between the two cultures, teaching us why we ought to listen to each other.

Preaching that is not touched by the doubts and questions of secular experience is not compelling. It loses touch with reality.

I have heard preaching that seems untouched by the doubts and questions raised by secular culture and experience, but it is not compelling. The preacher looks either a fool or a liar: too foolish to acknowledge the complex ambiguities of our experience, or pretending not to be affected by them. The preaching task in a postmodern context demands that the preacher have a rigorous conversation between her own questions and the resources of the Christian community: primarily the scripture, and also tradition, valued others, and the radically other (those with whom we profoundly disagree).

This places a demanding responsibility on preachers. We must be honest about our own doubts, questions, and experiences as we prepare to write. This part of the preaching task is confessional. The final sermon need not be autobiographical, but it must reflect the real issues and struggles of a person of faith. Preaching that seems to claim that the preacher never is plagued by questions will prove unhelpful to those who are, and it will give false comfort to those who insulate themselves from reflecting on such questions. Anti-intellectualism in the church is the direct result of preaching and teaching that glosses over important issues. Anti-intellectualism is immoral and contrary to the teachings of the gospel. And some of the most intelligent in our culture see it for what it is and stay home on Sundays to read Updike, because he is more honest.

Preachers need to be honest about their own doubts, their own questions, their own struggles, their own genuine affirmations, and the things they cannot affirm.

Another part of the preaching task is social inquiry. The preacher needs to hear the criticisms and concerns about a text or teaching from others who have a differing slant or opposing perspective than her own. Preachers need to make themselves aware of what other disciplines are offering as responses to life's pressing questions and to bring those disciplines into conversation with the claims of the gospel. Of course these extra-Christian claims must be criticized by the gospel mandate. But it is up to the preachers and teachers of the faith to show the connection between the gospel and the culture.

This leads directly to the exciting task of construction: building theological responses to questions that matter, offering ideas that liberate and energize and heal. I offer one more brief example of a sermon introduction that attempts to deal honestly with a problematic text. It names aloud the obviously troubling truth claims and invites the congregation to suspend disbelief long enough to enter into a different mode of language, a different kind of truth claim (tensive, poetic, postmodern). The sermon is on John's account of the raising of Lazarus (John 11:1-44).

An excerpt from a sermon on the raising of Lazarus illustrates how the preacher's honesty can coalesce with postmodern sensibilities in gospel witness. The sermon begins by acknowledging honest questions that are raised by the text. Indeed, the central affirmation of the text is outside the range of contemporary experience.

I have wondered how hard it would be today for some of us to hear this word of God, this gospel, this good news of the story of the raising of the man called Lazarus after four days in the grave. It is so far outside our experience. It stretches all credibility. We don't live in a world where people rise up out of graves—at least not outside of horror movies. We have come to accept strange near-death and life-after-death experiences on crash carts in the E.R. or in brightly lit operating rooms—but not in the graveyard.

In fact, for the children and youth here today, I've wondered if this story is just too creepy, too spooky, too scary to be good news. After all, you've likely seen lots of movies where people rise up out of graves, and in the movies, where it is never, ever good news! In Hollywood horror films this always means something bad is going to happen. It means something evil has been let loose on the earth. No, this story of a man wrapped up like a mummy and walking up out of a grave is hard for you young people to hear as happy, good news. And for those of you who are not feeling young at all these days—those of you who are feeling quite old, those of you who have too many aches and pains in your joints, who have made too many journeys to sickbeds, and you who have made too many sad journeys to funeral homes and cried by too many caskets—for you who would just as soon not look at death at all this morning, may I suggest a place to begin? For all of us who find this story hard to relate to, might I suggest a place where we can start to hear this story and let it work its healing power on us?

Start with Jesus, standing in a cemetery by the grave of a dear friend, someone he loves very much. Stand by Jesus, who is here in this cemetery with tears on his face, the wind tugging at his hair and robes. (Why is it that the wind is always so fierce in the cemetery?) Jesus is not alone here amidst the gravestones. He is standing with family and friends, with Mary and Martha and others. In fact, the whole world is standing here—standing by a grave and weeping. Many of us, indeed most of us have stood in the middle of a cemetery, in the middle of death. Most of us have stood right here, with tears streaming down our faces and wind tearing at our hair. *All* of us eventually will; which is why Jesus has come this day to the cemetery, to stand beside us and to cry with us in the face of death.

Here the sermon goes on to tell the story of a grieving family and a very present Christ. It concludes by attempting to use the scripture to imaginatively address some of the life issues that make best-selling titles for self-help books, bringing the gospel to bear on such issues.

What about that tomb? What about that dead body, that corpse lying there four days, already in decay? If you can, step with me into that tomb now. Take a look at the body, all wrapped up, protected and yet entrapped in bandages. Are you really sure it is Lazarus in there? *Or is it you?* Is that possible? For, you see, there is more than one way to die, and there is more than one kind of tomb. What if it may honestly be said that your existence is at times much like death and that you are even now in some profound sense entombed, entrapped, shut inside eternal darkness, your body already in decay? Perhaps your death trap is that ever-present fear of being found out: found out that you aren't quite as smart, or quite as good, or quite as happy as people think you are. This kind of fear gets inside your heart and eats away at you like some kind of cancer and renders you inca-

Being honest requires that we name our questions. This text requires that we admit our similarity to Lazarus. Sometimes we are entombed, awaiting a call to res-urrection.

pable of trusting anybody or of risking anything. And so you wrap yourself in bandages of self-protection. You close your-self in only to discover you are trapped in there. And you'd like to get out, but you don't have the power to roll away the stone, to rip off the bandages of fear and death and be set free! Or perhaps you are entombed in a sick and destructive relationship—love turned violent, passion turned to indifference, words once romantic now turned destructive. You've been wrapped in bandages of isolation and loneli-ness. You'd like to get out, but you don't know how.

Perhaps you are entombed by your job: a job that once held promise and purpose, a job where the money is good but the vocation—that profound purpose that God is calling you to is not there anymore, if it ever was. But the money and the health care and the security of that job have you wrapped up so tightly that you are mummified.

Or perhaps you are entombed by old habits or dead ideas or deathly prejudices, habits of the heart that have hardened toward destiny. Maybe it is the thought of death itself that entombs you: the fact of your own mortality, the limitations of the body.

Christ calls us out of our tombs. This call is not predicated on your knowledge or your power, but on the power of God in Christ. Do you hear Christ calling you?

You're searching desperately for a way to break out. You'd change these deadly fears or decaying relationships or deathly habits of the heart if you could. You'd change them if you knew how, but you don't. Just like Lazarus, you feel bound and gagged and decaying in that dark tomb of your life. Like Lazarus, your spirit seems to have left you there.

Whatever the shape of your tomb, hear today the voice of Jesus Christ calling you by name: "Come out!" Sitting in your dark tomb, can you make out that voice? We all have these tombs, these parts of our lives that entrap us and keep us from moving on. Sitting in your dark tomb, do you hear that voice? Can you see, amidst the darkness, an opening, a dim far-off light. Look now at that light. In the center of that light is a face. Eyes look at you with compassion: deep, compassionate eyes looking at you. He's calling to you now. Do you hear him? "Come out! Come out!" Something in you cries, "I can't. Christ, I can't! I want to but I don't know how." *But, this call is not predicated by your knowledge, or your power! This is about the power of God in Jesus Christ.*

So it doesn't matter that you don't know how. What matters is that you listen for that voice. And whatever the shape of your tomb, however dark your life is right now, look to the light and to that tear-stained face in the midst of the light. It is the love on that weeping face that will draw you out of your tomb by God's power, not by your own. Do you hear him calling?

Chapter Eight

Sample Sermons for a Postmodern Era

I n this chapter, Barbara, Scott, and Ron offer examples of preaching in a postmodern ethos. Each preacher attempts to incorporate philosophical and theological perspectives developed earlier in the book. The sermons are annotated to help the reader have a sense of what the preacher intended in the sermon as a whole and at important junctures in the sermon. These messages are not published as models for pastors to emulate, but as conversation starters. What seems to help each sermon speak in a postmodern setting? What seems to frustrate the sermon's capacity to communicate with postmoderns? As you think about your own preaching, what adjustments can you make to help your sermons relate better to an increasingly postmodern world?

A Sermon from Barbara Blaisdell

Beyond Being a Victim
Genesis 26:12-22; Romans 12:14-21

This sermon was preached to a largely postmodern congregation (one that includes, however, many moderns). It attempts to recover meaning and experience from an ancient biblical text and to provide mutual critical correlation between popular psychology (particularly insights from the Twelve-Step movement) and the Christian tradition.

I. Caught in the Crossfire

Today we are looking at the life of a forebear in the spiritual quest. I'm calling him the great middle patriarch. I call him that because the Jewish and Christian traditions are continually reminding us of our ancestors in the faith:

Abraham, Isaac, and Jacob. And our text for today focuses on the one in the middle: Isaac. Isaac isn't just named in the middle. He was the son of Abraham and the father of Jacob—the one in the middle generation. And his story is the story of someone caught in the middle throughout his life. His distinction seems to be that someone else is always doing something to him.

Isaac was born to a deeply religious couple late in their lives. And before he'd grown up, Isaac found himself caught between Abraham and his God. Indeed, his puberty found him on a mountain, tied to a pile of wood with his father's knife poised above his throat. His father convinced that this is what was needed to prove his piety, his devotion to God. Isaac would not be the last child put at risk by religious zeal. He did survive that incident, by God's intervention. On Isaac's fortieth birthday, when he was presumably old enough to make his own decisions, his father sent a slave to choose a wife for Isaac, a wife who, in his old age, would conspire against him. Rebekah was her name. She bore him two sons, Esau and Jacob, who in turn put their father Isaac in the middle of their sibling rivalry. This is a man who spent his life caught in the middle, caught in the crossfire of other people's passions, caught in the middle of other people's agendas.

In today's text, Isaac is caught in the age-old crossfire of politics and water rights. There was a famine in the land of Isaac's birth, so Isaac traveled west to the coastal lands of the Philistines. There he farmed the land and grew very wealthy. His neighbors were jealous. In their jealousy, they sent servants to fill with earth all of the wells in Isaac's birthplace—wells that his father had dug. And they came to him and asked him to leave their land. Imagine your neighborhood association meeting to take a vote to ask you to leave the neighborhood because you were a relative newcomer and too successful!

Have you ever felt caught in the crossfire? Caught in the middle of someone else's passions? Perhaps you know what it is to be caught in the middle of your parents' devotion to God, or their devotion to success, or to the American dream. And you felt sacrificed as a child, tied up in knots in the wilderness, left to find your own way home. Perhaps you've experienced the betrayal of neighbors and friends who saw some part of your life that looked good (no doubt better than you deserve), and in their jealousy they plug deep wells of good feeling and generosity that were the source of your life's goodness. Or perhaps you have been caught in the crossfire of a rivalry between peoples—siblings or parents or even strangers, as when, out of nowhere, someone pours out his fury at the world at you in the checkout lane of the grocery or in the office or in traffic on the way home. We can relate to Isaac, I suspect. We all know what it is to have our lives caught up in the struggles and conflicts not of our own making, fighting demons that we never invited inside us but who dwell there nevertheless.

II. Redigging Your Wells

That's why I love the story of Isaac and the wells. It is the story of one of the seekers of God successfully moving beyond his own victimization at the hands of the world. Recall the story. Recall that, because of a famine in the land of his birth, Isaac moved west to a land that was not empty, but already owned and occupied. And there, amidst the Philistines, he was allowed to settle as an immigrant. There, among the natives of that land, he worked hard and prospered, becoming even richer and more powerful than many of the native born. Now, it is hard but doable and gracious to let newcomers in. It is much harder to watch them prosper and flourish. And so the natives ask the immigrant Isaac to leave. And he does. He leaves and returns to the land of his birth, to the land where his father had immigrated and farmed and prospered. There he found his old wells filled with dirt—stopped-up; ruined. He responded by redigging them. He gave them back their original purpose—to provide water to a thirsty earth—and he gave them back their original names, the names that his father had given them.

There are some old wells in your life, some old sources of sacred waters that Philistine forces have filled up and blocked from you. Perhaps it's the well of worship and you have been blocked from drinking of its bounty by old wounds or current prejudices. Did you know that you have the freedom in Christ to redig those old wells; to clear out all the muck and grime put there by somebody else so that you can receive the fresh water of Christ's love? Maybe you have lost the deep and abundant wells of simple pleasures: a summer walk through a cornfield; the sight of a butterfly landing on Queen Anne's lace; the joy of hearing a new line of poetry so well written that your heart aches with the beauty of it. Have you lost that gift for joy in simple things? Has this culture's use of consumption as a "hit" or a "high" or a "fix" or your favorite form of entertainment polluted your capacity for pleasure in beauty outside the mall? Perhaps you need to redig the wells of your ancestors' simplicity: their Scottish thrift, or their Native American respect for mother earth, or their African respect for the beauty and wholeness of community. Did you know that you have the freedom in Christ to redig those old wells and learn again how to drink from the simple beauty of life?

One of our most sacred tasks in this place is to redig the abundant wells of scripture and tradition, to lift off the silt of old prejudice and confusion so that we can drink once again from its bounty. (We will, no doubt, knock some dirt of our own into the old wells—but more about that in a minute.) If you've been thirsting lately, perhaps for a deeper spirituality, the spirit of God is inviting you to redig some old wells.

Isaac doesn't stop, however, at redigging his daddy's old wells. He also discovers some new sources of sacred water. He happens upon these new sources while redigging the old sources. And he does not shy away from their newness. There are sources of the sacred that have not been discovered yet because God has put you and me here to discover them: new insights, new discoveries, new relationships. To be faithful means both to renovate those beloved old wells that have fallen into disrepair and to dig some new and original ones.

That's why it is so important that you ask your own questions, that you discern your own heart, that you pray in your own authentic way, that you use your own unrepeatable gifts to pursue your own true purpose. Don't stop drinking from the very best that your past has to offer. But also make certain you are drinking in new ways that are true to who you are here and now. Honor your past, but strive also for your own creative dream.

III. Whose Justice?

Back to our story: Here the plot thickens for Isaac (and for us). Isaac no sooner digs his own new well, than some herders arrive to inform him that it's their water. Isaac names the conflict for what it is. He calls the well *esek*, which means contention. And he moves on to dig another well. Here again the people of Gerar claim it as their own. And again Isaac names it for what it is: *sitnah*, hatred. And again he moves on. Do you begin to see a pattern here? Hard work, followed by outside interference, followed by conflict avoidance. Is Isaac a codependent wimp? Probably—in part. It's understandable that a child who barely survived his father's knife might have an aversion to violence, might well prefer a passive-aggressive

191

way to resolve conflict. On the other hand, the people of Gerar have a point. They were there first. Like the Philistines, they were the natives of that land. Isaac was a colonist, an interloper. Did he work to improve the land on which he settled? Yes! Does that hard work give him some rights? Yes! But it isn't that simple. Gerar was located in what is now known as the Gaza Strip—the very land and water under contention in the current Israeli/Palestinian peace negotiations. Land and water rights have never been easy to establish. Who is the victim here? Who is the oppressor? In our country, the controversy over property rights and environmental regulations represents the same moral ambiguity. Do I have the right to dig a well on my own land? Darn right I do. But what if my well lowers the water table, drying up the well of my neighbor?

In our scriptural passage, whenever Isaac is faced with this morally ambiguous problem, he gives in and moves on. Is scripture advocating that this ought always be our pattern—that every time people make a claim against us we ought to move on and let them have their way? That course will allow the bullies of this world to rule. Even pacifism is a morally ambiguous position. The lesson of Isaac is that there is no way to act in this complex and interrelated world so that you are always in the right, always above reproach, and never vulnerable to criticism. Isaac was, in a profound sense, a victim, having the fruits of his labor taken from him. But he was also a victimizer, his life and work inevitably encroaching on the life and work of others.

Have you ever prayed to God to get a certain job or to have a business deal go your way? Did you realize you were asking God not to give the job or the deal to someone else? There is no way to avoid this kind of moral dilemma. We live and breathe at the cost of others. And the unavoidable command for compassion to each and all—even those whose space we invade, even those who invade ours—will constantly be before us. Perhaps even worse, we can be our own victims. Too many of our wounds are self-inflicted. Too much of our lives are lived self-destructively, repeating old patterns because we are too afraid to live in a new way.

The question is not how to live a life above reproach, ten steps above criticism. We cannot. The question is, how can we live life graciously and beautifully amidst all of this moral ambiguity? Amidst the reality of our own sin? Amidst the reality of the unavoidable sin of others?

IV. Duck and Laugh

Let's look again at Isaac. He worked hard in the land of the Philistines and prospered. So they kicked him out. He worked hard again in the lands around the Gaza. And they pushed him out. He moved on to work hard again, to dig new wells. Is this a sign of co-dependence? Maybe. But it is far more than that. It's also an expression of undying hope, a willingness to persist on course despite resistance, a willingness to move ahead and move on when the cause is a lost one.

How does Isaac pull this off? Look again at his God. Look again to his name. Scripture and tradition refer to our God as the God of Abraham, of Isaac, and of Jacob. In Hebrew, our middle ancestor's name is pronounced Itzak, and it means laughter. Isaac means laughter. Abraham means many offspring or blessing. Jacob means striving or seizing of the dream, literally by the heel. And so our God, the God of Abraham, Isaac, and Jacob, is literally the God of blessing, the God of laughter, and the God of seizing the dream.

And Isaac—laughter—is in the middle. I think that's instructive for those of us caught in the middle. Suppose Isaac knew how to laugh in the middle of his predicament? His name would indicate that he did. How do you laugh at your own painful moral predicaments? Let me give you an example from my latest favorite writer: Anne

193

Lamott. She is writing here about a predicament not entirely of her own making. The father of her child has let her down, and therefore she is raising her son alone. Child rearing is hard work under the best of circumstances. Child rearing all alone can suck the life from you.

> I started feeling a little edgy about money or the lack thereof. I started feeling sorry for myself. . . . Pretty soon my self-esteem wasn't very good, and I felt that maybe secretly I'm sort of a loser. So when my friend John called a few minutes later from L.A. and mentioned that a mutual friend of ours, whose first book was out . . . had gotten a not-very-good review in Newsweek recently, all of a sudden, . . . I had a wicked, dazzling bout of schadenfreude. Schadenfreude is that wicked and shameful tickle of pleasure one feels at someone else's misfortune. . . . It made me feel better about myself. "Do you have it?" I asked innocently. . . . "Now read it." And when he was done, I said, "Man, that was like Christmas for me." Then we laughed, and it was okay for a minute.
>
> God, it was painful though, too, and the hangover was debilitating. I was deeply aware of the worm inside of me and of the grim bits that I feed it. The secret envy inside me is maybe the worst thing about my life. I am the Saddam Hussein of jealousy. But the grace is that there are a couple of people I can tell it to without them staring at me as if I have fruit bats flying out of my nose, who just nod, and maybe laugh, and say, Yep, yep, I get it, I'm the same. Still, I feel like it must drive Jesus just out of his mind sometimes, that instead of loving everyone like he or she is my sibling, with a heart full of goodwill and tenderness and forgiveness, I'm secretly scheming and thinking my dark greedy thoughts . . . I picture him stamping around like Danny DeVito, holding up these gnarled beseeching hands of frustration, saying, "Oy . . . veh."[1]

A soul secretly scheming, thinking greedy little thoughts. It's Anne. And yep, it's me. And yep, it's you, too. Every human soul is both victim and victimizer, oppressor and the oppressed. And nobody—*nobody*—

gets to identify him or herself so totally with the victim that it removes from us the command of God for compassion to each and all. Paul puts it this way: Bless those who persecute you, bless and do not curse them. Rejoice when they rejoice. Weep when they weep. Live in harmony, and do not claim to be wiser than you are. Do not repay evil for evil but strive/reach for what is best for all (Rom. 12:14-18ff.; my paraphrase).

And laugh in the midst of it. Laugh like Isaac and Anne at our silly, selfish selves, still loved by Jesus even as he says, *Oy veh!* And the God of Abraham, Isaac, and Jacob, the God of blessing, of laughter, and of striving for what is best—did you hear what this marvelous God will do?

Isaac finally dug a well, deep and pure and sacred, that he got to call his own. And he named it Rehoboth—literally, breathing space. God will make room for us. Oh, we will never manage to be above criticism. And life will never be fair—not this side of the grave. And there will always be more work for us to do. But if we persist and if we laugh with compassion for ourselves and others, God will grant us breathing space.

A Sermon from Scott Black Johnston

Inside, Outside, Upside, Down
Mark 4:1-23

This sermon was given during a weekly service of the Lord's Supper at Austin Presbyterian Theological Seminary during October 1995. The listeners were primarily seminary faculty members and students. This sermon was preached in the midst of numerous energetic and creative conversations going on within this community regarding postmodernity and its implications for the church (for instance, What is it? Can we embrace and learn from it? Or must we criticize and reject it?). While the sermon is not an explicit debate of these particular questions, it is clearly aware of such discussions, and accordingly, it seeks to speak a Gospel word that is attentive to postmodern people and issues.

While I was in high school,
visits by my Grandmother DeWolf
—my mother's mother—
always settled into the same comforting pattern.

Early in the morning
Grandma would descend on the kitchen,
wooden spoons and ceramic bowls rattling,
to stir up storm clouds of flour.
Her powerful arms were a whirlwind,
mixing, kneading and shaping
the pastries that were her hallmark.
    Before long,
    the odor of baked cinnamon and sugar
    would fill the house,
    tug me from my bed,
    and lead me unswerving to a table creaking under
    steaming breads and crusty pies.
    "Just look at him eat,"
    Grandma would say to my mother,
    as the poor woman attempted to restore order to her ravaged kitchen.
    "You can tell he's a DeWolf."
In that kitchen,
surrounded by generations and tradition,
I had a clear sense of identity.
I belonged with these people.
I was part of a family.
I was an insider.

The sermon begins by offering a picture of what it is to be an insider (i.e., safe, welcomed, and endowed with a clear sense of identity). I go on to unpack the first level of Mark's fourth chapter in a similar manner, noting how it invites listeners to adopt an insider pose when reading the text.

In the center of Mark's fourth chapter
there is a passage that beckons to us
like the incense of that kitchen.
Jesus has just told his first parable,
an agricultural tale
about a haphazard sower
and the fate of his widely scattered seeds.

Apparently, the parable comes off as a bit of a puzzler;
for the disciples, along with other close followers,
raise questions about it.
    Hearing their questions,
    Jesus gathers these folk around
    and makes an unexpected and powerful declaration.
        "To you has been given the secret
        (the mystery) of the kingdom of God,
        but for those outside everything comes in parables."
    It is an intriguing pronouncement
    —one that awakens our curiosity.
    There is a secret, a mystery, but what is it?
    There are insiders and outsiders, but who are they?
    All in all, it doesn't seem to require
    a Sherlock Holmes to figure it out.
Clearly, God's mystery is a gift,
something for disciples and followers
—people who are close to Jesus.
    They are the insiders.
Others are not close to Jesus;
they are hardened to God.
They *may* hear the words,
but they *will not* understand.
    They are the outsiders.
    Insiders. Outsiders.
    Inside they understand. Outside they don't.
    The text works on us.
    Insider? Outsider?
    "Which are you, gentle reader?"
    The answer may be easier than you think.
    Notice how Mark's Gospel pulls us close,
    providing us with the vantage point of the disciples.
    We sit with the select circle,
    overhearing as Jesus instructs and uplifts.
    We are placed in the position of followers.
    And so, the text reels us in . . .
    Can you smell the cinnamon and sugar?
    Here is a secure place
    —a spot next to Jesus—
    where you can participate in the mystery.
    You too can understand and be an insider.

197

After sketching a rather simple insider versus outsider dichotomy, the sermon invites the contemporary listeners to stand with the insiders—the disciples—around the teaching Jesus. Once this preliminary case for our status as insiders has been made, the sermon begins to narrow its focus by turning to a particular facet of the text—knowledge. Jesus seems to promise knowledge. But, knowledge of what? The Mystery? What kind of knowledge can you have of a mystery? Note how this question relates to our discussion of knowledge in chapter 4.

The text seems to promise
something that we desperately seek,
—especially here at seminary—
knowledge.
In this knowledge, the knowledge of the insider, lies security.
For to know the truth about God is
to be part of the elect—the chosen.

    Unfortunately, for those outside,
    Jesus doesn't seem inclined to expand the membership.
    In fact, his paraphrase of Isaiah,
      "They may indeed look, but not perceive,
      and may indeed listen, but not understand;
        so that they may *not* turn again and be forgiven"
    seems to sentence outsiders to eternal confusion.
One of the authors of the *Interpreter's Bible*
after trying—with increasing exasperation—
to make some sense of this passage,
finally argues Jesus could not possibly have said it.
Mark's take on the parables, he concludes, can only be termed "perverse."
    But wait, perhaps this interpreter could not hear the "hard" word.
    Maybe we just have to accept that God
    has selected some to understand (insiders),
    others not to understand (outsiders),
    and that's the way it is.
Our role, then, is to be faithful standard bearers,
the rightful keepers of God's mystery.
For we are the community who knows.

Many interpreters balk at the harsh nature of Jesus' words regarding outsiders. Some even conclude that this paraphrase of Isaiah was not spoken by Jesus and is instead the result of Mark's theological agenda. This debate obscures an important point. As the text of chapter 4 unfolds, what first seemed like a clear distinction between insiders and outsiders in vv. 10-12 is quickly blurred by Jesus in the pericope that follows. Noting this, the sermon follows the lead of the Marcan narrative to a second level of questioning. Are we sure that we are "insiders"? Do we really know the mystery?

In the short-story "Revelation,"
Flannery O'Connor describes a woman
who thinks that she has it all figured out . . .
culture, society, life itself.
    Mrs. Turpin,
    a pig farmer living in the south during the 1950s,
    has developed a grid for rating and ranking humanity.
    At the bottom of her hierarchy are the blacks,
    slightly above them she places the white trash.
    On the top of the pyramid are people just like Mrs. Turpin.
    White people. Polite people. Christian people.
    Mrs. Turpin's racism is only surpassed by her arrogance.
Then, at the height of her certainty,
this proud woman comes face-to-face
with a college student who looks beyond
polite manners and cheerful disposition
to point to the corruption that lies at Mrs. Turpin's core.
    With holy insight, this stranger calls Mrs. Turpin a "wart hog" and tells
her to "go back to hell."
    Suddenly seeing herself as a pig in another's eyes,
    Mrs. Turpin plunges to the bottom of the pile.
    This startling revelation overturns her world.
    The first has become the last, the last—the first,
    and her tidy hierarchy is flipped upside-down.
    Like Mrs. Turpin, we are not given the luxury
    of thinking that we have got it "all figured out" for very long.
    For, when we start to feel secure in the insider role,
    when we think that we have got

God's divine plan nailed down,
then we are vulnerable
to the alluring snare set by Mark's Gospel.
On the face of it,
Jesus seems to have clued-in the disciples:
"To you has been given the mystery of the kingdom of God."
But, if we think these followers have
suddenly reached a new level of understanding,
the text quickly lets us down.
    In the very next verse,
    a frustrated-sounding Jesus asks,
    "Do you *not* understand this parable?"
    —The simple one about the seeds?—
    "How will you understand all the parables?"
This is not the only time in the Gospel that Jesus chastises these folks.
In Mark, the disciples exemplify misunderstanding.
Again and again, they manage to miss the point.
Until, finally in chapter 8,
a weary Jesus asks,
    "Do you *still* not perceive or understand?
    Are your hearts hardened?
    Do you have eyes and fail to see?
    Do you have ears and fail to hear?
    And do you not remember?"
It all sounds familiar, except this time
the disciples play the role of the outsiders.
No longer is their place next to Jesus a secure one.
They *do not* understand the mystery.
    Teachings come to them
    wrapped in enigma,
    packaged as murky parables.

The poignant irony that unfolds as one reads Mark 4 is not lost on the contemporary listener. One moment the disciples are elbowing each other with confidence, and the next minute the teacher is handing out dunce caps. Just when listeners/readers think that they are in a position of security, Jesus gives a pop quiz. "Do you understand this parable?" The disciples, the characters with whom we have come to identify, fail this simple test. The sermon uses Flannery O'Connor's story to emphasize this reversal of fortune.

Like Mrs. Turpin, both the disciples and we, the readers, find our moments of theological certainty to be fleeting. From this point on, the sermon begins to question whether we are really promised security, certainty, and knowledge by Christ.

Do you recognize the scenario?
We, the faithful, come to seminary
seeking a deeper understanding of God's mystery.
We come believing,
(insiders expecting to find Grandma's kitchen)
and then we run into frightening questions,
unforeseen complications in the religious realm,
and we no longer feel at home.
      The faith that we once thought we had a handle on
      (we *knew* the mystery, we *were* the insiders)
      begins to slip through our grasp.
      Suddenly, everything flips upside down,
      and we are:
        the confused,
        the misunderstanding,
        the outsiders.
To spend time as an outsider,
as someone who cannot comprehend the mystery of God,
is a humbling experience.
And maybe it should be . . .
For too often we exhibit an arrogant confidence when it comes to God.
We know what team God would root for . . .
We know what political party God would vote for . . .
And we all—right, left, and center—
know where God stands on the ordination of homosexuals.
      But notice that Jesus does not say to the disciples,
      "You will *know* the secret."
      Jesus says, "You have been *given* (δέδοται) the mystery."
You have been given something that will not be controlled.
You have been invited to participate in something
that you cannot, at least for now, fully understand.
Now I see concern on some of your faces.
Does this text then repeal that classic, reformed slogan:
"Faith seeking understanding"?

Note how the following section of the sermon hearkens back to the chapter on knowledge. Certainly we should seek knowledge of God. But we must recognize the provisional character of that knowledge.

No, I don't think so,
but the text does provide us with a caution.
We are seekers of knowledge;
we are called by Christ to use every sense available
to listen and look and learn about the ways of our God.
We are students of the faith,
but we should never, never think
that we are truly "*Masters* of Divinity."
    So, we waver between inside and outside.
    And there is a good reason for that.
    For such is the character of our God.
Throughout the Gospel of Mark, one parable hovers over all the rest.
    In the midst of the disciples' fumblings and misunderstandings,
    the gospel continually pursues one mysterious question:
    "Who do you say that I am?"
An obscure English painter, Frank Dicksee,
has a single startling painting
hanging in the Tate Gallery in London.
The painting is entitled *The Two Crowns.*
In the center of the picture is a medieval king.
Decked out in bronze armor, wearing a jeweled crown,
he rides triumphant into a city on a white charger.
Crimson banners fly, trumpets are lifted,
young women strew pink rose petals along his path.
    Our attention is grabbed by the pageantry, the color, the splendor,
    and then, if we are persistent, by the king's eyes.
    Curiously, he is not looking at the adoring crowds
    but up to his left . . . beyond the festival.
    And then we see it.
    How could we have missed it?
    There on the fringe of the canvas,
    all in muted blacks and browns,
    is a crucifix, where another crown,
    one of thorns, sits on Christ's head.
The painting is a classic study of misdirection.
Our eyes are drawn to a central location,

missing crucial details on the periphery,
unless we notice the triumphant king's eyes.

The preceding illustration is reminiscent of our discussion of truth in chapter 3. Similar to our discussion of the absence of center, the Christ figure in this painting functions as a peripheral figure who calls the structures at the center of the artwork into question. One can detect a similar motif in the Gospel of Mark.

The Gospel of Mark functions in much the same way.
And the point of this scriptural misdirection
is not to occupy readers with a literary puzzle,
but to tell us something about the character of our God.
    So, while we look at the brilliant colors of the narrative,
    and speculate about the insiders and the outsiders,
    Mark's unswerving eyes are turned toward Jesus.
    On the fringes of the canvas we find the Christ,
    rejected by his home town,
    scorned by the religious establishment,
    and misunderstood by his closest companions.
    Redirecting our gaze,
    we suddenly see the true outsider.
I recently preached at a church
that has a ministry that it calls the "Joy Class."
The Joy Class is composed of mentally retarded adults
who attend worship each Sunday.
These folks sit together in the front pews,
warble incomprehensible phrases during the hymns,
and occasionally let out with a loud exclamation
to punctuate the preaching of the Word.
    When this particular service was finished
    (I preached on faith),
    one of the members of the Joy Class
    came to greet me with a hearty handshake.
    Then in humbling words that were difficult to decipher,
    he declared, "Faith, I don't believe in it."
All of a sudden, my definition
of "church" began to crumble.
I went in with the attitude that the most important
thing about Church was "knowing."

We Christians were a group of insiders,
  all pursuing knowledge of the same thing.
Yet, the words of one member of the Joy Class
tore the fabric of that assumption.
And in the face of that person,
a full member of the Christian community,
I caught a brief glimpse of our outsider God.
  The mystery of Jesus Christ has an unsettling demeanor,
  so that when we encounter it,
  when we are gifted with it,
  our limited expectations and finite structures are overturned.
In the end, this text reminds us
that Christ will not always be where we expect him to be,
a stationary object beneath our theological crosshairs.
  Instead, we worship something/someone infinitely more hopeful:
  a moving, mysterious God,
    who, in being active in the world,
    gives us a foretaste of a feast to come,
    who in refusing to be easily labeled,
    summons us to faithfulness.
A moving mysterious God
whose very character
calls us to also be outsiders in this world,
even while persistently beckoning us toward home.

A Sermon from Ronald Allen

Designing Deity
or
Why We Can Believe in God Today

The sermons from Barbara and Scott illustrate preaching with postmodern slants from biblical texts, whereas this is a topical sermon.[2] I chose a topical approach because the topic (belief in God) is broader than any single biblical text and because, as the sermon makes clear, the biblical communities were not concerned about the existence of God in the same way as contemporary communities. Although people with postmodern inclinations are often more receptive to the idea of transcendent reality than many moderns, a lot of postmoderns still want to know why they can believe in God.
  This sermon focuses only on possible rationales for believing that

God is. That agenda is sufficient for one sermon. The sermon indicates that this message would be one of a series focusing on other questions about God.

I review leading arguments for the existence of God from the premodern and modern worlds. In the end, however, I lay greatest stress on an argument from Charles Hartshorne that has a distinctly postmodern quality.

In the beginning of the sermon, I help the congregation focus on the importance of the topic by drawing on a personal life experience. I hope that many in the community can identify with the event and its questions. I attempt to show how the particular event relates to broader issues relative to the existence of God.

I was in high school in the 1960s.[3] Everyone in my family went to church. Without thinking much about it, we believed in the existence of God. And almost all of my friends went to church, too. Except for Charles. Charles is now a reporter. Every once in a while I see him on TV. But when we were growing up in a small town in the Ozark Mountains, he was the one person in my circle of friends who questioned whether there is a God.

Charles's favorite high school teacher was also our Sunday school teacher. I still remember the gasp that went through the Sunday school the day that Charles walked in the door. He sat patiently. But toward the end of the class, Charles raised his hand to speak: "Why do you believe in God? You can't see God. You can't hear God. You can't touch God." Some of the smartest young people in the high school were in that room. But we sat in awkward silence. The discomfort was relieved only by the bell.

One of our local television stations recently did a program on the fact that in the 1990s increasing numbers of people are turning to the church. In fact, a recent book calls the Baby Boomers, my group in society, "a generation of seekers."[4] Many people are searching for the meaning of life, and are finding help in the church and in

God. One woman said she is returning to church because, "There's just got to be more than I am."

That discovery is wonderful. But the assertion by itself may not be enough to support faith. Charles's question opens a window of uncertainty. If you can't see, hear, or touch God, what makes you think God is there?

So, I want to think with you about why it is possible to believe in God. One sermon cannot begin to answer all our questions about God. Consequently, this is the first in a series of message on God. In the next weeks, I will focus on God's character and purposes, on how we can know God, on how God works in the world, and on God's relationship with evil. But, those sermons all rest on the one today.

The sermon now turns to the Bible. Since Scripture is a primary authority in the Christian community, the church should always consult it for possible perspectives on important issues. This section aims to elucidate the guidance the Bible can (and cannot) offer concerning the existence of God. The turn to the Bible also taps postmodern respect for the past.

You might expect that we could get help from the Bible. And people in the world of the Bible had many of the same questions about God that we do. What is God's nature? What are God's purposes? What does God ask? What does God promise? On what can we count from God? What does it mean to be faithful to God? One of the purposes of the Bible is to clarify the character, activity, and requirements of the God of Israel.

But there is an important difference between people in the world of the Bible and us. As far as we know, almost everyone in the ancient world believed in some kind of deity. In fact, most people in antiquity believed that the world was full of gods (little g) and other superhuman forces. There were almost no atheists or agnostics. So, one of life's central questions was: Which deity(ies) do you serve? Apollo? Zeus? Osiris? The God of Israel?

The Bible does not speculate about why it is possible to believe. The Bible explains why it is important to serve the God of Israel. On this question, the Bible is not as helpful to us as it is on some other questions.

The sermon now takes up how the church (and some outside the church) have cognitively formulated rationales for God's existence. I follow Charles Hartshorne in identifying several key arguments for the existence of God. In a short sermon, I can only sketch broad outlines of arguments that are particularly clear and compelling. Hartshorne notes that all these arguments have weaknesses, and that no single argument is persuasive by itself.[5] In the postmodern spirit of critical evaluation, I hope the congregation can get a sense of the strengths and weaknesses of these arguments. I also hope the community discovers the plurality of reasons for trusting in God.

Reason ↓

After the Bible was written, some people began to question the reality of God. Over the centuries, Christians have articulated several famous "arguments" to postulate the existence of God.[6]

Of course, you cannot "prove" the existence of God in the same way that you can prove that 2 + 2 = 4. God is not an object that we can manipulate and measure. But if you have an inclination to believe, you can come to rational reasons for believing. Anselm, a leader in the church in the eleventh century, speaks of "faith seeking understanding." You want to believe. You may not be able to "prove" God, but you can have the confidence that it makes sense to believe in God. Or, a friend of mine says, you can conclude that it is not irrational to believe.[7]

I refer to these lines of reasoning as arguments (and not proofs). Arguments are persuasive. But they do not estab-

lish indisputable fact. These arguments can help you
believe that it is intellectually credible to believe.

A contemporary philosopher says that if he were asked,
"Why do you believe in God?" he would not reply that he
believes because of any single argument. "Rather, I would
say that it is because of a group of arguments that mutually
support one another so that their combined strength is . . .
like that of a cable whose strength sums the strengths of its
several fibers."[8]

One of the oldest arguments was articulated by Plato and
Aristotle. Good company.[9] It is called the cosmological argument because it reasons from the existence of the world, the
cosmos, to the existence of God. It goes like this. The world
exists. The existence of the world implies the existence of a
first cause. Without a first cause, the process that made the
world would not have started. Christians call the first cause
God.

Another approach is called the argument from design.
Or, its more formal name is the teleological argument.[10]
The word *telos* means end or goal. The idea is that the
universe exhibits design and order. The various parts relate
to one another so as to maintain life. The intricacy of this
working together could not be an accident. It results from
a Designing Deity, God.

People often develop this argument without any formal
training in philosophy. I have often heard Sunday school
teachers marvel at how the human body has everything
that it needs to function. The argument can be extended
from the design of the cell to the design of the universe.
"This world couldn't be so complete by accident!"

According to the aesthetic argument, the beauty of the
universe can be accounted for by an artistic God. On a
summer night, you lie on your back and look up at the
deep canopy of space. You are overwhelmed by the beauty of the world and by how everything fits together. You

think that it had to be designed to fit together so well. And so you conclude that there must be a Master Artist, God.

As its name implies, the moral argument is based on moral experience. Human beings are aware, innately and intuitively, of moral commands. We know certain things are right and certain things are wrong. The presence of moral commands presumes a commander. However, "the commander cannot be the individual human moral agent, for what today I command myself to do, I can tomorrow command myself not to do. I can have absolute moral obligations only if a God exists to command them."[11]

My favorite argument for believing in God, and the most persuasive argument that I know, was developed by Anselm and refined by the contemporary North American thinker, Charles Hartshorne.[12] The other reasons that I have discussed largely depend upon observation of life. You look at some aspect of life—its design, the fact of its existence, its beauty, the presence of moral intuition—and you conclude that the existence of God is the most rational explanation for those things. But Anselm's argument is rooted in the process of thinking itself.

With nothing more than reasoning, you can come to a rational conclusion that God exists. Here is how. Anselm says that God is the greatest imaginable being. You cannot conceive of a being greater than God. A being greater than God is unimaginable. The very idea of God includes every possible good and perfect characteristic. We would all say that it is better, more perfect, to exist than not to exist. (After all, which is better, which would you rather have: a real, existing chocolate ice cream cone, or an imaginary one?) Therefore, from the very idea of God we can conclude that God must really exist, because it is more perfect to exist than not to exist.[13]

Now, all of these arguments have weak spots. The design of this world is not always so wonderful or reliable. And sometimes the world is not very beautiful. Natural disasters. Tensions in human relationships. Fatal diseases. Big fish eat smaller fish. And some say that Anselm demonstrates that thinking about God's existence implies nothing more than the *thought* of God's existence. But taken together, these different arguments have a cumulative effect. So, while the arguments do not prove God, they do show that it is *reasonable* to believe in God. Or, as I said a moment ago, these arguments show that it is not unreasonable to believe in God.

Furthermore, I am encouraged in another way by these arguments, and by others that I have not mentioned. They come from intelligent people. People whom I respect stand on the sensibility of these arguments, even as they acknowledge that the arguments have their weak points. These are people with good minds, whose questions penetrate to the bare wood, who look the toughest questions in the eye and do not flinch. Sometimes, frankly, I am in church meetings in which people say and do things that are embarrassing; I want to crawl into the nearest cold air return and hide. But the company of the authors of these arguments is company whom I am pleased to keep.

To this point, the sermon has focused on traditional arguments for the existence of God. The message now briefly explores some representative practical effects of the confidence that God exists. The focus is on a concern that is important to postmoderns—our experience. In this part of the sermon I speak a lot in the first person singular pronoun, but I intend that it function as a representative, communal "I" as discussed in chapter 5.

Now, to be honest, these arguments do not directly show that the First Cause, the Designing Deity, the Great Artist, the Supreme Commander is the God of Israel and of Jesus Christ, the God of love and justice. The week after next, the sermon will address how we can know the character and purposes of God. But for now, it is enough to realize that these arguments add up to the credibility of belief in such a God.

Furthermore, it makes sense to think that God is present and active in my experience and in yours. And believing in God helps us make sense of our experience. Believing in God helps me understand things that happen to me. Things that I think. Things that I feel.

The Lord's Supper. The sanctuary is quiet, but it is not silent. The rattle of the trays as they are lifted from the table. The clink of the tiny communion glasses. The soft tearing of pieces of bread from the loaf. The quiet tap of the deacons' shoes on the tile floor. The organ stops. I take the bread and the cup. I hold them in my hands. Pastor Riley speaks the words of institution. I put them to my lips. And I feel a fullness, an overflowing goodness. I sense the presence of Another. A wondrous love whose depths I can only imagine. And I can believe that Someone really is there.

emotion

Confidence in God's existence is more than comfort. It also means that I am responsible to Someone who knows me better than I know myself—including the secrets of my heart that are so shameful or frightening that I hide them even from myself, and the attitudes and actions that betray me. Yes, I stand before a judge whose court needs no rules of evidence. For the judge has X-ray vision and perfect recall of every time and situation.

The actuality of this One who knows all means that every one of my thoughts and actions makes a difference. Even when I am by myself. What I think and what I do can bring joy or sadness to God. Uttering a thank you under my breath when I get good news is not just talking to myself.

I close the sermon by recounting an incident involving a parishioner with whom I hope the congregation can identify. I

211

hope the lawyer's story brings together experience and logic in a compelling way to help confirm the possibility of belief in God on the part of the postmodern listeners. This story serves as an "evidential experience" (as described on p. 64).

At the time the sermon was prepared, the O. J. Simpson trial was in the daily news. People were very aware of the rules of evidence as the prosecutors and the defense attorneys wrangled over what was admissible and what was not. That seemed to give a timely quality to the references to evidence in this story.

Not long after my spouse and I began a copastorate in Nebraska, one of our parishioners, an attorney and a leader in the congregation, invited me to lunch. He wanted to talk with me about believing in God. He described his extensive training in logic, argument, debate, and evidence. He said that he had struggled for years with whether or not to believe that God exists. "I take a role in the church. I pray at the Lord's Table. I teach Sunday school. I bring my wife and children. Now, if God doesn't exist, I'm a liar. And I'm leading other people in a lie. And, actually, I'm helping them waste time they could be using more constructively to help themselves and to help other people. There are some Sunday mornings when Merry [his wife] and I would like to walk around our lake, and get some exercise, and pick trash out of the water so the fish won't choke on it. But, instead, we come to church. I thought to myself, 'Either God exists, or this God thing is a big hoax and I need to get away from it for my own sake and for the sake of the people I am misleading.' "

After a long pause I asked him "What tipped the scale?"

"I was looking for the smoking gun. Finally, it dawned on me that you believe in God on the basis of circumstantial evidence. I can't bring God into court for questioning. But it makes logical sense to think that something like God is behind all this." He gestured to the world around us. "I'm putting my integrity on the line to believe. It gives my life a whole added dimension—to think that I am living not just for myself, but for God."

I like the way William James thinks about these things.[14] He says that it is not irrational to believe. The arguments for the existence of God, the experiences that we have—these assure us that our faith makes sense. I join my attorney-parishioner friend and stake my integrity on God. I hope you will too.

Introduction

1. For representatives of the range of definitions, see Margaret Rose, *The Postmodern and the Post-Industrial* (Cambridge: Cambridge University Press, 1991), esp. pp. 3-20.
2. Charles W. Allen, "Contemporary Theology" (unpublished paper).

1. What Does Postmodernism Have to Do with Preaching?

1. For complexities in the premodern world, see Huston Smith, *Forgotten Truth: The Primordial Tradition* (Harper & Row, 1976).
2. William C. Placher, *Unapologetic Theology* (Louisville: Westminster/John Knox Press, 1989), p. 26, from whom I draw this characterization.
3. Many theorists associate general public recognition of post-modernism with the publication of Jean-Francois Lyotard, *The Postmodern Condition: A Report on Knowledge*, trans. Geoff Bennington and Brian Massumi (1979; reprint, Minneapolis: The University of Minnesota Press, 1984).
4. David Ray Griffin, *God and Religion in the Postmodern World* (Albany: State University of New York Press, 1989), p. x.
5. Griffin, *God and Religion in the Postmodern World*, p. x.
6. Clark M. Williamson, "Confusions in Disciples Talk and Practice: Theology in the Life of the Church," *Discipliana* 55 (1955), p. 5.
7. Stanley Hauerwas and William Willimon, *Resident Aliens* (Nashville: Abingdon Press, 1989), p. 24.
8. Clark M. Williamson, "Confusions in Disciples Talk and Practice."
9. Griffin, *God and Religion in the Postmodern World*, p. xi.

10. Ibid.
11. David Tracy, *On Naming the Present: God, Hermeneutics, Church* (Maryknoll: Orbis Books; London, SCM Press, 1994), pp. 14-15.
12. Dean R. Hoge, Benton Johnson, and Donald A. Luidens, *Vanishing Boundaries: The Religion of Mainline Protestant Baby Boomers* (Louisville: Westminster/John Knox Press, 1994), p. 112.
13. Charles Taylor, *The Ethics of Authenticity* (Cambridge: Harvard University Press, 1991), pp. 16-17.
14. Jean-François Lyotard, *The Postmodern Explained* (Minneapolis: University of Minnesota Press, 1992), p. 16.
15. Karl Barth, *Word of God and Word of Man*, trans. Douglas Horton (Gloucester, Mass.: Peter Smith, 1978), p. 108.

2. Authority in the Pulpit in a Postmodern Ethos

1. Lyman T. Lundeen, "The Authority of the Word in a Process Perspective," *Encounter* 36 (1975), p. 281.
2. On the distinction between *de facto* and *de jure* authorities, see Stanley I. Benn, "Authority," *The Encyclopedia of Philosophy*, ed. Paul Edwards (New York: The Macmillan Co., 1967), vol. I, pp. 215-18.
3. On the development of the notion of authority, see Hannah Arendt, "What Was Authority?" in *Authority*, ed. C. J. Fredrich (Cambridge: Harvard University Press, 1958), pp. 81-112.
4. Ibid., pp. 98-99.
5. William C. Placher, *Unapologetic Theology* (Louisville: Westminster/John Knox Press, 1989), p. 26.
6. Ibid., p. 29.
7. Edward Farley, *Ecclesial Reflection* (Philadelphia: Fortress Press, 1982), pp. 165-70.
8. This notion of authority, deriving from a sense of promise for human and cosmic life, is similar to viewpoints in feminist and process theologies as well as in some liberation theology. For an example of feminist thought, see Letty M. Russell, *Household of Freedom: Authority in Feminist Theology* (Philadelphia: The Westminster Press, 1987), pp. 17-20. For

persuasive authority, see Alfred North Whitehead, *Process and Reality*, corrected edition, ed. David Griffin and Donald Sherburne (New York: The Free Press, 1978), pp. 342-43.

9. Of course, the gospel can be formulated in different ways. However the gospel is formulated, Paul Hanson points out that a community of faith needs a transcendent theological vision within which to make sense of particular texts, doctrines, claims, and practices. See his *Dynamic Transcendence* (Philadelphia: Fortress Press, 1978), p. 74. My statement of the gospel attempts to provide such a vision. The particular notion of the gospel as an ellipse with two foci is drawn from Albrecht Ritschl, *The Christian Doctrine of Justification and Reconciliation*, transl. by H. R. Mackintosh (New York: Charles Scribner's Sons, 1900). As the subtitle suggests, for Ritschl the two foci are justification and reconciliation. The idea that the two foci of the gospel are love and justice is adapted from James A. Sanders's analysis of the constitutive and prophetic hermeneutical axioms that guided Israel's interpretation and reinterpretation of its faith. For example, see James A. Sanders, *Canon and Community* (Philadelphia: Fortress Press, 1984), p. 52. The universal quality of this formulation of the gospel ("for each and all") is derived from the monotheizing tendency that Sanders finds characteristic of biblical writers. The emphasis on love as the center of the gospel is consistent with my own tradition, the Christian Church (Disciples of Christ). See Alexander Campbell, *The Christian System*, 4th ed. (Cincinnati: H. S. Bosworth, 1870), who says that we read the Bible, and all Christian affirmations, ". . . with the eyes of the understanding fixed solely on God himself, his approbation and complacent affection for us" (p. 17). Another of my theological ancestors, Barton Stone, speaks of divine love at the center of his conversion. Stone heard a preacher speak of "The love of God to sinners, and of what that love had done for sinners." Upon hearing that testimony, "Stone's heart warmed with love for that lovely character described." See Elder John Rogers, *The Biography of Eld. Barton Warren Stone, Written by Himself: With Additions and Reflections* (Published for the author by J. A. and U. P. James, 1874), reprinted in Hoke S.

Dickinson, ed. *The Cane Ridge Reader* (n.p. 1872), pp. 10-11. For further elaboration of this formulation of the gospel, see Clark M. Williamson and Ronald J. Allen, *A Credible and Timely Word* (St. Louis: Chalice Press, 1992), pp. 6-7, 71-77; see also Williamson and Allen, *The Teaching Minister* (Louisville: Westminster/John Knox Press, 1991), pp. 75-81.

10. Huston Smith, *Forgotten Truth: The Primordial Tradition* (New York: Harper & Row, 1976).

11. Delwin Brown points out that tradition also contains a vast body of nonconscious but immensely powerful feelings. See his *Boundaries of Our Habitations: Tradition and Theological Construction* (Albany: State University of New York Press, 1994), pp. 46-54.

12. Williamson and Allen, *The Teaching Minister*, pp. 65-82; Williamson and Allen, *A Credible and Timely Word*, pp. 71-76.

13. For such a method, see chapter 5, pp. 119-21.

14. Some modern thinkers anticipate these ideas (e.g., Schleirmacher, whose notion of experience included suprarational elements).

15. Bernard E. Meland, *Fallible Forms and Symbols* (Philadelphia: Fortress Press, 1976), p. 54.

16. See note 13.

17. Hans-Georg Gadamer, *Truth and Method*, trans. and ed. Garrett Barden and John Cumming (New York: Crossroad Publishing, 1982), pp. 330-31.

18. David Tracy, *Plurality and Ambiguity* (San Francisco: Harper & Row, 1987), p. 30.

19. Ibid., p. 19.

20. I do not generally recommend spoken give-and-take between preacher and congregation (or among members of the congregation) in the sanctuary. My experience of such events is largely negative.

21. Reuel Howe, *Partners in Preaching* (New York: Seabury Press, 1967), p. 53.

22. Ibid., p. 47.

23. John McClure, *The Round Table Pulpit* (Nashville: Abingdon Press, 1995).

24. Charles Taylor, *The Ethics of Authenticity* (Cambridge: Harvard University Press, 1991), pp. 31-32.

25. Hannah Arendt, "What Is Authority?" *Between Past and Future*, ed. C. J. Fredrich (New York: Viking Press, 1968), p. 91.

26. Mark C. Taylor, *Erring: A Postmodern A/Theology* (Chicago: University of Chicago Press, 1984), p. 87. Cf. Acts 3:15.

27. For a contemporary proponent of this position, see E. D. Hirsch, Jr., *The Aims of Interpretation* (Chicago: University of Chicago Press, 1976).

28. Taylor, *Erring*, p. 16.

29. Ibid., p. 6. This conclusion is reached by both Taylor and his mentor in the methods of deconstruction, Jacques Derrida.

30. Fred B. Craddock, *As One Without Authority* (Nashville: Abingdon Press, 1971), p. 2.

31. Ibid., p. 14.

32. Stanley Fish, *Is There a Text in This Class? The Authority of Interpretive Communities* (Cambridge: Harvard University Press, 1980), pp. 322-27.

33. Richard Sennett, *Authority* (New York: Random House Publishers, 1980), p. 197. Sennett, a sociologist who has studied authority, seems to agree with Fish. He writes, "Authority is itself inherently an act of imagination. It is not a thing; it is a search for solidity and security in the strength of others which will seem to be like a thing."

34. Cf. Arendt, "What Is Authority?" p. 93. Here Arendt points out the derivative nature of the concept. "Authority is given by another; it is not taken through coercion."

35. Letty M. Russell, *Household of Freedom: Authority in Feminist Theology*, pp. 43-57.

36. Cf. St. Augustine, *Contra Epistulam Fundamenti* c. 410, 2. He writes "I would not have believed the gospel had not the authority of the church moved me."

3. Truth in the Postmodern World

1. A. N. Prior, "Correspondence Theory of Truth," *The Encyclopedia of Philosophy*, ed. Paul Edwards (New York: Macmillan Publishing and The Free Press, 1967), vol. 2, pp. 223-32.

2. These two approaches seem to me to be most characteristic of the modern period. In the nineteenth century, the pragmatic theory (holding that the true is that which works) also came to expression. See Gertrude Ezorsky, "Pragmatic Theory of Truth," *The Encyclopedia of Philosophy*, vol. 6, pp. 427-30. The performative theory of truth is a kind of bridge between modern and postmodern notions; see also Ezorsky, "Performative Theory of Truth," *The Encyclopedia of Philosophy*, vol. 6, pp. 88-90.

3. Alan R. White, "Coherence Theory of Truth," *The Encyclopedia of Philosophy*, vol. 2, pp. 130-33.

4. Michel Foucault, *Power/Knowledge: Selected Interviews and Other Writings, 1972-1977*, trans. Colin Gordon (New York: Pantheon Books, 1980), p. 131, cited in Clark M. Williamson, "Confusions in Disciples Talk and Practice: Theology in the Life of the Church," *Discipliana* 55 (1995), pp. 4-5.

5. Nancy Fraser, "Michel Foucault: A 'Young Conservative'?" *Ethics* 96 (1985), p. 172, cited in Williamson, "Confusions in Disciples Talk and Practice," p. 5.

6. For leading postliberal assessments of different approaches to truth, see George Lindbeck, *The Nature of Doctrine* (Philadelphia: The Westminster Press, 1984), pp. 47-52, 64-66; and William C. Placher, *Unapologetic Theology* (Louisville: Westminster/John Knox Press, 1989), pp. 121-37.

7. However, note that William Placher argues that there can be persuasive reasons for accepting the Christian story. In *Unapologetic Theology*, pp. 134-35, Placher seems to adopt a modified version of truth as correspondence in a position similar to the one I adopt below.

8. Bernard Meland, *Fallible Forms and Symbols* (Philadelphia: Fortress Press, 1976), p. 54.

9. Ibid., p. 43.

10. For an exceptional exposition of this position, see David Ray Griffin, "Liberation Theology and Postmodern Philosophy: A Response to Cornel West," in *Varieties of Postmodern Theology*, ed. by David Ray Griffin, William A. Beardslee, and Joe Holland (Albany: State University of New York Press, 1989), pp. 133-41.

11. That would be naive foundationalism. Foundationalism was a modern philosophical emphasis that sought to identify the pure, uninterpreted facts of experience, the foundations on which reality was built. Foundationalism has taken a severe beating at the hands of philosophers in the postmodern period. For a concise overview of foundationalism and its representatives and opponents in theology in the late modern and early postmodern periods, see Douglas F. Ottati, "Between Foundationalism and Nonfoundationalism," *Affirmation* 4 (1991), pp. 27-47.

12. Alfred North Whitehead, *Process and Reality*, corrected ed., ed. David Ray Griffin and Donald W. Sherburne (New York: The Free Press, 1978), p. 151.

13. Hans Van Der Geest, *Presence in the Pulpit*, trans. Douglas W. Stott (Atlanta: John Knox Press, 1981), pp. 114-21.

14. Charles Birch, *A Purpose for Everything* (Mystic, Conn.: Twenty-Third Publications, 1990), p. 125.

15. Joseph Sittler, *The Care of the Earth and Other University Sermons* (Philadelphia: Fortress Press, 1964), pp. 75-88.

16. A concise introduction to mutual critical correlation can be found in the works of David Tracy, esp. *Blessed Rage for Order* (New York: Seabury Press, 1975), and *The Analogical Imagination* (New York: Crossroad Publishing 1981).

17. On this notion see further Clark M. Williamson and Ronald J. Allen, *A Credible and Timely Word* (St. Louis: Chalice Press, 1991), pp. 96-98.

18. The first two rubrics are adapted from suggestions by James A. Sanders (though Sanders does not discuss them in relationship to postmodernism). See his *Canon and Community* (Philadelphia: Fortress Press, 1984), p. 73.

19. Jacques Derrida, *Writing and Différence*, trans. Alan Bass (Chicago: University of Chicago Press, 1978), p. 279.

20. Martin Heidegger, *Being and Time*, trans. John Macquarrie and Edward Robinson (San Francisco: Harper & Row, 1962).

21. Derrida, *Writing and Difference*, p. 279.

22. Ibid., p. 280. As Derrida puts it, we look for "full presence which is beyond play."

23. Ibid., p. 279.
24. Mark C. Taylor, *Erring: A Postmodern A/Theology* (Chicago: University of Chicago Press, 1984), p. 6.
25. Ibid., pp. 174-75.
26. Derrida, *Writing and Difference*, pp. 295, 297, 300.
27. Karl Barth, *The Epistle to the Romans*, trans. E. C. Hoskyns (Oxford: Oxford University Press, 1968), p. 35.
28. Karl Barth, *Das Wort Gottes und die Theologie*. Gesammelete Vortsaege. Band 1. (Muenchen: Chr. Kaiser Verlag, 1925), p. 158. This translation was suggested by W. Stacy Johnson.
29. Eberhard Jüngel, "Metaphorical Truth: Reflections on the Theological Relevance of Metaphor as a Contribution to the Hermeneutics of Narrative Theology," in his *Theological Essays* (Edinburgh: T & T Clark, 1989), p. 16.

4. Preaching as a Source of Knowledge

1. John Calvin, *Institutes of the Christian Religion*, ed. John T. McNeill, trans. Ford Lewis Battles (Philadelphia: The Westminster Press, 1950), vol. 1, p. 35.
2. A very readable survey is D. W. Hamlyn, "Epistemology, History Of," in *The Encyclopedia of Philosophy*, ed. Paul Edwards (New York: Macmillan Publishing 1967), vol. 3, pp. 8-38.
3. O. A. Piper, "Knowledge," *The Interpreter's Dictionary of the Bible*, ed. George A. Buttrick et al. (Nashville: Abingdon Press, 1964), vol. 3, p. 43.
4. John T. McNeill, in John Calvin, *The Institutes of the Christian Religion*, vol. 1, pp. 35-36, note 1.
5. The image of knowledge as bricks is drawn from Arthur Koestler, *Bricks to Babel: Selected Writings with Author's Comments* (London: Picador Press, 1982), cited in Charles Birch, *A Purpose for Everything Under Heaven* (Mystic, Conn.: Twenty-Third Publications, 1990), p. 126.
6. As pointed out in chapter 1, some moderns were sympathetic to the knowledge that could come from feeling. One thinks particularly of Schleirmacher and some of the romantic poets.
7. Birch, *A Purpose of Everything Under Heaven*, p. 139.

8. Susanne K. Langer, *Problems in Art* (New York: Charles Scribner's Sons, 1957), p. 15.

9. Alfred North Whitehead, cited in Bernard Meland, *Fallible Forms and Symbols* (Philadelphia: Fortress Press, 1976), p. 50.

10. Bernard Meland, *Fallible Forms and Symbols*, p. 24.

11. Alfred North Whitehead, cited in Meland, *Fallible Forms and Symbols*, p. 29.

12. Michael Polanyi, *The Tacit Dimension* (Garden City, N.Y.: Anchor Books, 1967), p. 4.

13. Aidan Kavanaugh, "Teaching Through Liturgy," *Notre Dame Journal of Education* 5 (1974), p. 43.

14. Fred B. Craddock, *As One Without Authority*, 3rd ed. (Nasvhille: Abingdon Press, 1979), p. 78.

15. For a helpful guide to this aspect of preaching, see Henry Mitchell, *Celebration and Experience in Preaching* (Nashville: Abingdon Press, 1990).

16. Mark C. Taylor, *Erring, A Postmodern A/Theology* (Chicago: University of Chicago Press, 1984), p. 7.

17. Ibid., p. 6.

18. *Erring*, p. 6. It is a rather disconcerting sight, for, according to Taylor, "an a/theology that draws on deconstructive philosophy will invert established meaning and subvert everything once deemed holy." See also Jacques Derrida, *Positions* (Chicago: University of Chicago Press, 1981), p. 40. It should be noted that at certain points Derrida seems to doubt that any sort of connection between theology and deconstruction is possible. For the primary concept around which deconstruction revolves *(différence)* "blocks every relationship to theology."

19. *Erring*, p. 11.

20. Ibid., pp. 168-69.

21. See Jacques Derrida, *Writing and Differénce*, trans. A. Bass (Chicago: University of Chicago Press, 1978), p. 298. While not referring to grace, Derrida describes the human condition in a similar manner, i.e., as being plunged "into the horizontality of pure surface."

22. *Erring*, p. 169. Taylor goes on to state: Mazing grace opens "a

way of totally loving the world, and not only a way of loving the world, but also a way of [writing] love itself in a time and world in which God is dead." In this description, Taylor borrows from one of the original figures of the "death of God" movement, Thomas J. J. Altizer. See Altizer's "Eternal Recurrence and the Kingdom of God," in *The New Nietzsche*, ed. D. B. Allison (New York: Delta Books, 1979), p. 245.

23. *Erring*, p. 176. Are we compelled by contemporary literary theory to turn cherished concepts like grace into multi-leveled descriptions of the futility of the human condition?

24. Ibid., p. 150. It is this uncertain climate, Taylor claims, that makes his project possible. "The time and space of graceful erring are opened by the death of God, the loss of self, and the end of history."

25. See ibid., pp. 9-10. Taylor writes that theology refuses to allow the possibility that "oppositional terms can coexist peacefully." Deconstruction provides "a critical lever" for disorganizing this inadequate binary approach to concepts.

26. John Calvin, *Institutes of the Christian Religion*, vol. 2, ed. John T. McNeill, trans. Ford L. Battles (Philadelphia: The Westminster Press, 1960), p. 3032, "Therefore, since the whole Christ is everywhere, our Mediator is ever present with his own people, and in the Supper reveals himself in a special way, yet in such a way that the whole Christ is present, but not in his wholeness. . . . Now if anyone should ask me how this takes place, I shall not be ashamed to confess that it is a secret too lofty for either my mind to comprehend or my words to declare. And, to speak more plainly, I rather experience than understand it."

27. I have adapted a phrase made popular by David Kelsey, *To Understand God Truly: What's Theological About a Theological School* (Louisville: Westminster/John Knox Press, 1992).

28. Karl Barth, *Church Dogmatics*, trans. by Geoffrey Bromiley (Edinburgh: T & T Clark, 1956), vol. IV/2, pp. 124-25.

29. For a homiletician who recognizes the importance of holding together grace and judgment, see Paul Scott Wilson, *The Practice of Preaching* (Nashville: Abingdon Press, 1995), pp. 106, 118, 154-55, 162, 186.

5. Preaching About God in a Postmodern Setting

1. For overviews of positions, see Langdon Gilkey, "God," in *A New Handbook of Christian Theology*, ed. by Donald W. Musser and Joseph L. Price (Nashville: Abingdon Press, 1992), pp. 198-209.
2. E.g., Schubert Ogden, *The Reality of God* (New York: Harper & Row, 1963), p. 177. Cf. Charles Wesley, "Love Divine, All Loves Excelling," *Chalice Hymnal* (St. Louis: Chalice Press, 1995), p. 517.
3. Clark M. Williamson, "Preaching the Gospel: Some Theological Reflections," *Encounter* 49 (1988), p. 191. For a fuller account of this notion of the gospel, see chapter 2, note 9.
4. See further Clark M. Williamson, *A Guest in the House of Israel* (Louisville: Westminster/John Knox Press, 1993), pp. 22-25.
5. Norman Pittenger, *Freed to Love* (Wilton, Conn.: Morehouse-Barlow Publishers, 1987), p. 117.
6. For further discussion of these notions, see Ronald J. Allen and John C. Holbert, *Holy Root, Holy Branches: Christian Preaching from the Old Testament* (Nashville: Abingdon Press, 1995), pp. 124-28; cf. Williamson and Allen, *A Credible and Timely Word*, pp. 107-9.
7. Professor Williamson made this statement in personal conversation.
8. These are developed further in Clark M. Williamson and Ronald J. Allen, *A Credible and Timely Word* (St. Louis: Chalice Press, 1991), pp. 71-129; and Williamson and Allen, *The Teaching Minister* (Louisville: Westminster/John Knox Press, 1991), pp. 65-82.
9. For critique of intelligibility, see Stanley Hauerwas and William Willimon, *Resident Aliens* (Nashville: Abingdon Press, 1989), pp. 19-24.
10. For possible configurations of hermeneutical relationships, see Williamson and Allen, *A Credible and Timely Word*, pp. 91-129.
11. This proposal, obviously, is a modified version of demythologizing. It is developed further in Williamson and Allen, *A Credible and Timely Word*, pp. 96-97.

12. For a fuller assessment of such difficult passages, see Ronald J. Allen and John C. Holbert, *Holy Root, Holy Branches*, pp. 128-31.
13. *Chalice Hymnal*, p. 1.
14. Karl Barth, *Church Dogmatics*, trans. by G. T. Thompson (Edinburgh: T & T Clark, 1936), vol. I/1, pp. 371-72.
15. Ibid., p. 371. "All we can know of God according to the witness of Scripture are His acts. All we can say of God, all the attributes we can assign to God, relate to these acts of His; not, then, to His essence as such."

6. Individual and Community in Postmodernity

1. For a penetrating study of the notion of community in Israel and in the early church, see Paul D. Hanson, *The People Called: The Growth of Community in the Bible* (San Francisco: Harper & Row, 1986).
2. J. W. Rogerson, "Corporate Personality," in *The Anchor Bible Dictionary*, ed. David Noel Freedman et al. (Garden City: Doubleday, 1992), vol. I, pp. 1156-57.
3. E.g., Exodus 14:1-31; Deuteronomy 28; Joshua 10:12-13; 1 Kings 17:8-16; Psalm 65:9-13; Isaiah 11:6-9; 35:1-2; 55:12-13; Joel 1:19-20; Jonah 1:17–2:10; Habakkuk 3:8-4; Matthew 27:45-54; Mark 1:12-13; Luke 19:28-40; Acts 16:25; Romans 8:18-25; Revelation 6:12-17.
4. Of course, prophets regularly arose who critiqued the modern world.
5. Some in the modern world, of course, regarded nature in a nonutilitarian way; for instance, Henry David Thoreau, and the romantic poets.
6. For explorations on community in postmodernity, see *On Community*, ed. Leroy S. Rouner (Notre Dame, Ind.: University of Notre Dame Press, 1991).
7. Similar visions are found in other streams of thought, such as forms of feminism, some liberation perspectives.
8. E.g., Alfred North Whitehead, *Process and Reality*, corrected ed., ed. Donald W. Sherburne and David R. Griffin (New York: The Free Press, 1979), p. 50. For development, see

Catherine Keller, *From a Broken Web* (Boston: Beacon Press, 1986), pp. 182-88.

9. Keller, *From a Broken Web*, p. 184.

10. Ibid.

11. See Whitehead, *Process and Reality*, p. 43.

12. Marjorie Suchocki, *God, Christ, Church*, rev. ed. (New York: Crossroad Publishing Co., 1992), pp. 78-79.

13. For examples of views of the cosmos that move in this direction, see Alfred North Whitehead, *Modes of Thought* (1938; reprint, New York: Capricorn Books, 1958), pp. 173-232; Charles Hartshorne, *Creative Synthesis and Philosophic Method* (Lasalle, Ill.: Open Court Publishing Co., 1970), pp. 141-43. In the last fifteen years, environmental concerns generated a vast body of literature, e.g., Charles Birch and John B. Cobb, Jr., *The Liberation of Life* (Cambridge: Cambridge University Press, 1981); *The Reenchantment of Science*, ed. David Ray Griffin (Albany: State University of New York Press, 1988); Jay B. McDaniel, *Of God and Pelicans* (Louisville: Westminster/John Knox Press, 1989); *Liberating Life: Contemporary Approaches to Ecological Theology*, ed. Charles Birch (Maryknoll: Orbis Books, 1990); Ronald Nash, *Loving Nature* (Nashville: Abingdon Press, 1991); John Haught, *The Promise of Nature* (Mahwah: Paulist Press, 1993); James Gustafson, *A Sense of the Divine: The Natural Environment from a Theocentric Perspective* (Cleveland: Pilgrim Press, 1994).

14. Stanley Hauerwas and William H. Willimon, *Resident Aliens* (Nashville: Abingdon Press, 1989), pp. 50-51, 78, 91.

15. Ibid., p. 46.

16. Ibid., p. 47.

17. For a magisterial postliberal reply to such criticisms, see William C. Placher, *Unapologetic Theology* (Louisville: Westminster/John Knox Press, 1989), pp. 166-70.

18. For a thorough answer to criticisms of the postliberal vision of the relationship of the church and the culture, see Stanley Hauerwas and William H. Willimon, *Where Resident Aliens Live* (Nashville: Abingdon Press, 1996).

19. H. H. Farmer, *The Servant of the Word* (1942; reprint, Philadelphia: Fortress Press, 1964), pp. 43-44.

20. The most notable exception to this trend is David G. Buttrick, *Homiletic* (Philadelphia: Fortress Press, 1987), who specifically develops a homiletic for communal consciousness.

21. The African American community has retained vital elements of communal identity. However, leading interpreters of African American life indicate that excessive individualism is beginning to corrode parts of African American life.

22. Thomas C. Oden, "Can We Talk About Heresy?" *The Christian Century*, April 1995, (112); pp. 390-403.

23. There is some question as to who first coined the term "post-Christian," but W. Stacy Johnson points to H. Richard Neibuhr's early use of this category in his fourth Cole Lecture at Vanderbilt University in 1961. See: H. Richard Niebuhr, *Theology, History, and Culture*, ed. William Stacy Johnson (New Haven: Yale University Press, 1996), p. xxi.

24. Perhaps the most famous example of this is Stanley Fish, *Is There a Text in This Class? The Authority of Interpretive Communities* (Cambridge: Harvard University Press, 1980).

25. Feminist theologians have also exhibited considerable interest in community and church. Certainly the tack taken by scholars such as Letty Russell diverges in significant ways from the figures treated in this section, but feminist theology does share a common tenet with Hauerwas et al.; for both invest considerable authority in community.

26. Karl Barth, *Church Dogmatics*, vol. 1, trans. G. T. Thomson (Edinburgh: T & T Clark, 1936), pp. 3-4. From the very first page of his magnum opus, Karl Barth declares that "theology is a function of the church." Shortly thereafter, Barth again points to the church's central role in his theological method by stating: "The church produced theology in this special and peculiar sense by subjecting itself to self-examination." Cf. Hans W. Frei, *Types of Christian Theology*, ed. George Hunsinger and William C. Placher (New Haven: Yale University Press, 1992), pp. 38-46.

27. *New Testament: Contemporary English Version* (New York: American Bible Society, 1991).

7. Modes of Discourse for the Sermon in the Postmodern World

1. Anthony C. Thistleton, "The Supposed Power of Words in the Biblical Writings," *Journal of Theological Studies* 25 (1974), pp. 283-99. I am grateful to Paul Franklyn for pointing me to this article.

2. For a survey of contemporary understandings of language, see Stephen W. Littlejohn, *Theories of Human Communication*, 4th ed. (Belmont, Calif.: Wadsworth Publishing, 1992).

3. For a review of terminology and uses, see Ronald J. Allen, "Shaping Sermons by the Language of the Text," in *Preaching Biblically*, ed. Don M. Wardlaw (Philadelphia: The Westminster Press, 1983), pp. 29-34.

4. Philip Wheelwright, *The Burning Fountain: A Study in the Language of Symbolism* (Bloomington: Indiana University Press, 1954), pp. 25-29, 55-59.

5. Philip Wheelwright, *Metaphor and Reality* (Bloomington: Indiana University Press, 1962), p. 46.

6. For representative literature, see Allen, "Shaping Sermons by the Language of the Text," pp. 29-34.

7. See Peter L. Berger and Thomas Luckmann, *The Social Construction of Reality* (1966; reprint, Garden City, N.Y.: Doubleday Anchor Books, 1967), pp. 34-46; cf. Ronald J. Allen, "The Social Function of Language in Preaching," in *Preaching as a Social Act*, ed. Arthur Van Seters (Nashville: Abingdon Press, 1988), pp. 167-204.

8. Susanne K. Langer, *Philosophy in a New Key* (Cambridge: Harvard University Press, 1942), pp. 71-101.

9. Susanne K. Langer, *Feeling and Form* (New York: Charles Scribner's Sons, 1953), p. 292.

10. A clear exposition of this aspect of Ricoeur's thought is Ted F. Peters's "Hermeneutics and Homiletics," *Dialog* 21 (1982), pp. 121-29.

11. A few biblical texts or other elements of Christian tradition are so problematic that the preacher cannot reappropriate them. The sermon ought preach against them. For criteria for making such a judgment, see chapter 5, pp. 119-21.

12. My view here is functionally similar to that of some postliberals. For an exceptionally concise statement of the latter, see William C. Placher, "The Nature of Biblical Authority: Issues and Models of Recent Theology," in *Conservative, Moderate, Liberal*, ed. Charles R. Blaisdell (St. Louis: CBP Press, 1990), pp. 11-15.

13. For a detailed approach to the sermon which invites the preacher to take into account these multiples of factors, and that touches on postmodern concerns, see Paul Scott Wilson, *The Practice of Preaching* (Nashville: Abingdon Press, 1995).

14. For representative typologies of differences in the ways in which people receive and process information, note the following. James W. Fowler, *Stages of Faith* (San Francisco: Harper & Row, 1981); Isabel Myers Briggs and Peter M. Briggs, *Gifts Differing* (Palo Alto, Calif.: Consulting Psychologists Press, 1993); Richard Bandler and John Grinder, *Frogs into Princes* (Moab, Utah.: Real People Press, 1979), vol. 2, pp. 1-26; Mary Belenky et al., *Women's Ways of Knowing* (New York: Basic Books, 1986); William G. Perry, Jr., *Forms of Intellectual and Ethical Development in the College Years* (New York: Holt, Rinehart, and Winston, Inc., 1970); Robert Kegan, *The Evolving Self* (Cambridge: Harvard University Press, 1983); Kegan, *In Over Our Heads* (Cambridge: Harvard University Press, 1994).

15. For a model of analyzing congregational life, see Don M. Wardlaw, "Preaching as the Interface of Two Social Worlds: The Congregation as Corporate Agent in Preaching," in *Preaching as a Social Act*, pp. 55-94. For a review of the literature of congregational studies, see Allison Stokes and David A. Roozen, "The Unfolding Story of Congregational Studies," in *Carriers of Faith*, ed. Carl S. Dudley, Jackson W. Carroll, and James P. Wind (Louisville: Westminster/John Knox Press, 1991), pp. 183-92.

16. Fred B. Craddock, *As One Without Authority* (1971; reprint, Nashville: Abingdon Press, 1979).

17. Edmund Steimle, Morris Niedenthal, Charles Rice, *Preaching the Story* (Philadelphia: Fortress Press, 1980).

18. Eugene Lowry, *The Homiletical Plot* (Atlanta: John Knox Press, 1980).

19. Henry Mitchell, *Celebration and Experience in Preaching* (Nashville: Abingdon Press, 1990).

20. David G. Buttrick, *Homiletic* (Philadelphia: Fortress Press, 1987).

21. Note the essays in Don Wardlaw, ed., *Preaching Biblically*; cf. David G. Buttrick, *Homiletic* (Philadelphia: Fortress Press, 1982), pp. 333-65; Thomas G. Long, *Preaching and the Literary Forms of the Bible* (Philadelphia: Fortress Press, 1988); Sidney Greidanus, *The Modern Preacher and the Ancient Text* (Grand Rapids: Eerdmans, 1988). From a historical-critical perspective see Ronald J. Allen, *Contemporary Biblical Interpretation for Preaching* (Valley Forge: Judson Press, 1984), pp. 49-59.

22. Paul Scott Wilson, *The Imagination of the Heart* (Nashville: Abingdon Press, 1988). Cf. Charles L. Rice, *Interpretation and Imagination* (Philadelphia: Fortress Press, 1970).

23. Thomas H. Troeger, *Imagining a Sermon* (Nashville: Abingdon Press, 1990).

24. Clyde E. Fant, *Preaching for Today*, rev. ed. (San Francisco: Harper & Row, 1987); Richard F. Ward, *Speaking from the Heart* (Nashville: Abingdon Press, 1992).

25. John McClure, *The Round Table Pulpit* (Nashville: Abingdon Press, 1995); cf. William E. Dorman and Ronald J. Allen, "Preaching as Hospitality," *Quarterly Review* 14 (1994), pp. 295-310.

26. Ronald J. Allen, *Preaching the Topical Sermon* (Louisville: Westminster/John Knox Press, 1992).

27. Frederick Buechner, *Whistling in the Dark: An ABC Theologized* (New York: Harper & Row, 1988), p. 107.

28. Stanley Hauerwas, "The Church as God's New Language," in *Scriptural Authority and Narrative Interpretation*, ed. Garrett Green (Philadelphia: Fortress Press, 1987), p. 179.

29. See Thomas G. Long, "Living with the Bible," in *Homosexuality and the Christian Community*, ed. Choon-Leong Seow (Louisville: Westminster/John Knox Press, 1966), pp. 64-73.

30. I am informed on this point by William Greenway, "Christian Ethics in a Postmodern World? Hauerwas, Stout and Christian Moral *Bricolage*," *Koinonia*, vol. VI, no. 1 (Spring, 1994), pp. 1-31. The Christian *bricoleur*, as cast by Greenway, recognizes the provisional nature of knowledge, yet continues to work with the Christian narrative to try and piece together faithful responses to moral dilemmas. In many ways, my position in this book advocates that we think of the preacher as a homiletical *bricoleur*.

31. Thomas G. Long, *The Witness of Preaching* (Louisville: Westminster/John Knox Press, 1989), p. 106. "A good sermon form, then, grows out of the particularities of preaching this truthful word on this day to these people" (p. 105). Cf. Karl Barth, *Church Dogmatics*, trans. Geoffrey W. Bromiley (Edinburgh: T & T Clark, 1936), I/1. "The question is not how [a person] in general and as such can know God's Word. This question is pointless, for vis-à-vis the Word of God there is no [person] in general and as such; the Word of God is what it is as it is concretely spoken to this or that specific [person]" (p. 196).

32. Fred Craddock, *Preaching* (Nashville: Abingdon Press, 1985), p. 25.

33. Christine M. Smith, *Preaching as Weeping, Confession, and Resistance: Radical Responses to Radical Evil* (Louisville: Westminster/John Knox Press, 1992), pp. 1-2.

34. John McClure, *The Round Table Pulpit: Where Leadership and Preaching Meet* (Nasvhille: Abingdon Press, 1995). Cf. Leonora Tubbs Tisdale, *Preaching as Local Theology and Folk Art* (Minneapolis: Fortress Press, 1996).

35. Thomas G. Long, "And How Shall They Hear? The Listener in Contemporary Preaching," in *Listening to the Word: Studies in Honor of Fred B. Craddock*, ed. Gail R. O'Day and Thomas G. Long (Nashville: Abingdon Press, 1993), p. 187.

36. Craddock, *Preaching*, p. 19.

37. John Updike, *In the Beauty of the Lilies* (New York: Alfred A. Knopf, 1996), p. 5.

38. Ibid., p. 75.

8. Sample Sermons for a Postmodern Era

1. Anne Lamott, *Operating Instructions: A Journal of My Son's First Year* (New York: Fawcett Columbine, 1993), pp. 120-21.
2. See Ronald J. Allen, *Preaching the Topical Sermon* (Louisville: Westminster/John Knox Press, 1992).
3. I thank Charles R. Blaisdell for helping me sort through the issues and literature related to this sermon.
4. Wade Clark Roof, *A Generation of Seekers* (San Francisco: HarperCollins, 1993).
5. Charles Hartshorne, *Creative Synthesis and Philosophic Method* (La Salle: Open Court Publishing, 1970), pp. 275-97. For a systematic discussion, see Donald Wayne Viney, *Charles Hartshorne and the Existence of God* (Albany: State University of New York Press, 1985).
6. I apologize to philosophically sophisticated readers for oversimplifying these arguments. Perhaps the sermon could be followed by educational events that explore these basic ideas.
7. This observation is from Charles R. Blaisdell (personal correspondence), drawing on William James, "The Will to Believe," in his *The Will to Believe, Human Immortality, and Other Essays on Popular Philosophy* (New York: Dover Publications, 1956), pp. 1-31.
8. Charles Hartshorne, "Foreword," in George W. Goodwin, *The Ontological Argument of Charles Hartshorne*. American Academy of Religion Dissertation Series 20 (Missoula, Mt.: Scholars Press, 1978), p. xi.
9. For a concise discussion, see Ronald W. Hepburn, "Cosmological Argument for the Existence of God," in *The Encyclopedia of Philosophy*, ed. Paul S. Edwards (New York: Macmillan Publishing, and The Free Press, 1967), vol. 2, pp. 232-37.
10. For a concise discussion, see William P. Alston, "Teleological Argument for the Existence of God," in *The Encyclopedia of Philosophy*, vol. 8, pp. 88-92.
11. Ronald W. Hepburn, "Moral Arguments for the Existence of God," in *The Encyclopedia of Philosophy*, vol. 5, p. 382.

12. According to Charles Hartshorne, Anselm developed two arguments for the existence of God. In this sermon, for the sake of brevity, I follow Hartshorne's development of the second argument. Hartshorne discusses this argument in many of his writings, e.g., *Anselm's Discovery* (Lasalle, Ill.: Open Court Publishing, 1965), esp. pp. 85-98.

13. Ibid., p. 34. Hartshorne's emphasis. I owe this interpretation of the Anselm-Hartshorne approach to Charles Blaisdell.

14. William James, "The Will to Believe."

Index